To The
MEMORY OF THE PIONEERS
OF
THE OHIO COUNTRY
THE OLD NORTHWESTERN AND SOUTHWESTERN TERRITORIES
OF THE UNITED STATES OF AMERICA
THIS BOOK
IS RESPECTFULLY DEDICATED

THE OHIO COUNTRY
Between the Years 1783 and 1815

Including
Military Operations that Twice Saved to the
United States the Country West of the
Alleghany Mountains after the
Revolutionary War

Charles Elihu Slocum, M.D., Ph.D., LL.D.
Member of Local, Ohio State, and American Historical Associations

The War of 1775–1783 between the United Colonies and Great Britain, was Revolutionary; The War of 1812–1814 between the United States and Great Britain, was the War of Independence.

HERITAGE BOOKS
2010

HERITAGE BOOKS
AN IMPRINT OF HERITAGE BOOKS, INC.

Books, CDs, and more—Worldwide

For our listing of thousands of titles see our website at
www.HeritageBooks.com

A Facsimile Reprint
Published 2010 by
HERITAGE BOOKS, INC.
Publishing Division
100 Railroad Ave. #104
Westminster, Maryland 21157

Copyright © 1910 Charles Elihu Slocum

— Publisher's Notice —
In reprints such as this, it is often not possible to remove blemishes from the original. We feel the contents of this book warrant its reissue despite these blemishes and hope you will agree and read it with pleasure.

International Standard Book Numbers
Paperbound: 978-1-55613-473-9
Clothbound: 978-0-7884-8335-6

PREFACE

THE early and most trying times in the history of the Old Northwestern Territory, and of its great neighbor, the Southwestern Territory, divided only in a physical sense by the Ohio River, is a subject that should ever be of interest, and of value to everyone, of every land, especially as a study in patriotic endurance.

The story presents people strong in brain and in brawn, descendants of Anglo-Saxon and of Celtic stocks, the ancestors of most of whom had been several generations in America, having originally settled here one hundred and fifty years before; a people who loved their new homes in the forest country as well as the homes of their nativity in the Colonies along the Atlantic shore, now separated from their early habitat by several hundred miles, and by mountains hard to traverse.

This isolated people were often made to feel that they and their new country were forgotten by the legislators and others in authority in the regions whence they came; and during many years their struggles were not alone for subsistence, but for the protection of themselves and their children from prowling Savages, who were seeking their scalps and lives, or to drive them from their adopted country.

In preparing this book the writer has had in mind the general reader who wants a direct account of the subject about which he desires to read, with enough of detail for supplementation, when such detail is obtainable.

Such readers have generally noticed that histories of the United States, even the largest ones, when mentioning this extensive and invaluable region at all, give a very scant account of the dangers which would have attended its loss to the American Union, or of the military operations that twice, at least, saved it to, and maintained it in, the Union.

In writing it is easier, for several reasons, to generalize than to focus one's attention on the detail that shows the animating principle, or want of principle, that influenced the lives, thoughts, acts, and accomplishments of the people. This statement may explain how it is that many write so much and yet impart so little of practical information.

Preface

The character of the sufferings of Americans, before the Revolutionary War and for thirty years after, in this trans-Allegheny region particularly, exacts strong language even in its mildest portrayal.

The tragic story here written has, however, a very pleasant conclusion for Americans. At its beginning, naught but dark clouds of selfishness and savagery hung low in the horizon, frequently bursting out into storms that caused great suffering and disaster, and that would have overfatigued and driven from the country, never to return, the survivors, had they possessed less strong and self-reliant characters.

Disagreements among the Eastern Colonies, and later among the States into which these Colonies were transformed, occasionally foreboded evil to the union of the Ohio Country with the East and, at times, even foreboded disruption of the Union among the States themselves.

However, the War of 1812–1814 came, and ended, as a blessing to both the East and the West, in that it consolidated, and cemented, the States and Territories into a nation with not only valuable experiences, but with heightened and reciprocated regard for one another instilled into the ·component parts, and with greater forbearance, improved ideals and powers among all.

True civilization receives impetus from the lessons of the past. History should be truthfully and fully written, even though its pages record horrible deeds.

The habitual use of intoxicating beverages was a strong factor in much of the savagery recorded in the following pages, as well as being the cause of the inefficiency of several Americans in authority during this time, of the older military commanders particularly.

By reading, and keeping in mind, an authentic account of the trials and sufferings of the early settlers in gaining and maintaining liberty from oppression and savagery, people are more likely to appreciate liberty gained in this way, and to remain more intent upon its preservation.

CHARLES E. SLOCUM.

TOLEDO, OHIO.

CONTENTS

CHAPTER I

INTRODUCTION 1

The Settling of the British and French in America—Their Inebriation of the Aborigines—Made them Savages Indeed—Habitual Contention for Ascendancy—Success of the British with the Savages, and against the French—Use of Savages against Colonists during Revolutionary War by the British the same as against the French in Previous Years.

CHAPTER II

BRITISH DIRECT NON-OBSERVANCE OF TREATY OF PARIS, AND THEN SIGN THE TREATY 18

The First Years Following the Revolutionary War—The First Northwestern Boundary Line—The Aborigines Willing to be Friends of the United States—Causes of their Alliance with the British—The British Continue to Hold Military Posts in Opposition to Treaty—Large Amount of American Property Purloined by the British.

CHAPTER III

DEVELOPMENT OF THE WEST CHECKED BY BRITISH INFLUENCES. 33

Aborigine Claims to Land Based on Conquest, which Claims the Savages and the British were

Not Willing to Accede to the United States, their Conqueror—Treaties with Aborigines—Reservations—Cession to United States of Western Claims by States—Civil Organizations—Surveys for Settlements—Ohio Land Companies—Fort Finney Built—Continued Control of Aborigines by British—Expeditions against Savage Marauders—Desire in the West for Independence from the United States—Unauthorized Retaliations on Spaniards Allayed.

CHAPTER IV

CONTINUED NEFARIOUS WORK WITH THE SAVAGES 42

Activities of the British against the United States—Their Main Fort in American Territory Strengthened—Benedict Arnold with them—Organization of the Territory Northwest of the Ohio River—Increase in Population—Other Civil Organizations—More Systematic Efforts to Check British Influence with American Aborigines—Forts Built—Reports of the extensive Savage Work Done by the Aborigines—Cannibalism.

CHAPTER V

FURTHER CULMINATION OF THE INEFFICIENT MANAGEMENT OF AFFAIRS 52

Statement of the Conditions by Jurist from Personal Observations—Necessity for Relieving the Long-continued and Severe Sufferings—Kentucky Territory Organized—Other Civil Organizations—General Harmar's Expedition against Hostile Savages at Head of Maumee River—His Army Twice Defeated by them—Their Celebration of Victory at Detroit with

Contents   xi

PAGE

their British Allies—Panic along Frontier—The
Weak, Inefficient American Conduct of Affairs
Reviewed.

CHAPTER VI

OVERWHELMING SUCCESS OF THE ENEMY   62

More Troops Gathered for Defence—Messenger
Sent to the Senecas for Peace Agents—British
Opposition—Expedition against Hostile Savages Successful—Army Gathered for Decisive
Blow to the Marauding Savages—Commanded
by General, and Governor, St. Clair, it Meets
Overwhelming Defeat—Women with the Army.

CHAPTER VII

FURTHER NEFARIOUS WORK CULMINATING   78

Great Efforts of British Allies—Distress of Frontier
Settlements—British Fear Loss of Fur Trade—
Advance of Civil Jurisdiction—General Wayne
Chosen to Lead Another Army against the
Hostiles—Further Treaties with the Aborigines
—Secret Efforts to Learn Status of the British—
Largest Council of Savages for British Confederation—Kentucky Admitted as a State—Forts
Built by Americans—Commissioners Appointed
to Attend the Great Council—Their Object
Defeated by the British—Specific Charges of
Fraud and Force by British Presented to the
British Minister.

CHAPTER VIII

RETRIBUTIVE JUSTICE MARCHES ON AGAINST
GREAT OPPOSITION   95

Advance of General Wayne's Army—Opposed
by the Enemy—Builds Forts Greenville and

Recovery—Cause of British Aggressiveness yet More Apparent—Other Enemies of the United States—Separation of the Ohio Country from the United States again Suggested—British Build Two Additional Forts within United States Territory—Protests of the United States of No Avail—British and their Savage Allies Attack Fort Recovery and Are Repulsed—Further Account of Great Britain's Guiding Hand.

CHAPTER IX

WAYNE'S ARMY DEFEATS A HYDRA OF CONSPIRACIES 108

Further Advance of Wayne's Army—A Most Momentous Campaign—Builds Forts Adams and Defiance—The Enemy Flees—Wayne's Last Overture for Peace—The Army Nears the Enemy—Builds Fort Deposit, and Advances to Complete Victory—Buildings and Crops of British and their Allies Destroyed—Wayne's Emphatic Letters to the Commandant of Fort Miami—The Casualties—Army Returns and Strengthens Fort Defiance—The Red Savages—British Strengthen their Forts in United States Territory.

CHAPTER X

THE TAMING OF THE BROKEN SAVAGE SPIRIT 121

Wayne Marches his Army to the Site of the Miami Villages—There Builds Fort Wayne—Receives and Makes Valuable Friends of Deserters from the British—Disaffection of Kentucky Volunteers—They are Sent Home—Savage Scouts Active at Fort Defiance—Wayne's Suggestion of General Council with Aborigines Meets Favor.

Contents xiii

PAGE

CHAPTER XI

THE MOST IMPORTANT OF ALL TREATIES WITH
THE SAVAGES 131
   Discipline in the Army—Wayne's Diplomacy in
   Winning the Savages to Peace—His Agents in
   the Work—Exchange of Prisoners—The Treaty
   of Greenville, August 3, 1795—Number of
   Tribes in the Agreement.

CHAPTER XII

THE WEST GAINS POSSESSION OF PART OF ITS
RIGHTS 144
   Treaty with Spain Favorable to the West—Abandonment of Forts—British again Endeavor to
   Seduce the Aborigines of the United States—
   The Jay Treaty Favorable to the West—British
   Surrender American Forts—Death of General Wayne—Wayne County Organized—More
   French and Spanish Plots—Separation of the
   West from the East again Suggested—British
   Threaten Spanish Possessions in the South.

CHAPTER XIII

ADVANCEMENT OF CIVIL GOVERNMENT, AND EXTENSION OF THE WEST 156
   Mississippi Territory Organized—General Washington again at the Head of the Federal Army
   —Spanish Surrender their Forts in United
   States Territory—First Legislature of Northwestern Territory Convenes—Indiana Territory
   Organized—Public Lands—Connecticut Cedes
   her Claims to the United States—Religious
   Missionaries — Population — Continued British
   Usurpations—Evidences of the Rising Power
   of the United States—Treaty with France—

Louisiana Territory Purchased—Development of Communication—Military Posts—Ohio Admitted as a State—The Aborigines—Additional Treaties with them—Fort Industry Built—Michigan Territory Organized—Aaron Burr's Last Scheme.

CHAPTER XIV

Conspiracy of the British, Tecumseh, and the Prophet 167

Further Treaties with, and Payments to, the Aborigines—The British Continue Meddlesome—Reservations—United States Settlers by the Lower Maumee River—Land for Highways Treated for—Illinois Territory Organized—Another British-Savage Trouble Gathering—Trading Posts for the Aborigines Established—Reports of Gathering Trouble from United States Military Posts—The British Continue to Trade Intoxicating Liquors to American Aborigines in Opposition to Law.

CHAPTER XV

Results of Further Remissness of the Government 180

Regarding Trading Posts or Agencies—Conspiracy of the British and Tecumseh Deepens—Reports from Military Posts—Battle of Tippecanoe—Continued Organization and Depredations by the Allied Enemies of the United States—Missouri Territory Organized—More Cannibalism by the Savages.

CHAPTER XVI

Sad Beginning of the War for Independence 194

Tardy Action of Congress—Declaration of War against Great Britain—This War of 1812 the

Contents xv

PAGE

Real War for Independence—The Army of the Northwest the First in the Field—Forts McArthur, Necessity, Findlay, and Miami Built—Sad Inefficiency of General Hull—He Orders the Abandonment of Fort Dearborn—Massacre and Cannibalism by British Allies—Hull Surrenders Fort at Detroit without Effort for Defence—Brave and Patriotic Work by Captain Brush.

CHAPTER XVII

SLOW PROGRESS IN PREPARING TO MEET THE ENEMY 204

Efforts to Repair Hull's Loss—General Harrison Appointed Commander-in-Chief—Siege of Fort Wayne Relieved—General Winchester Appointed to Succeed Harrison without Cause.

CHAPTER XVIII

EXTREME SUFFERINGS OF KENTUCKY SOLDIERS 212

General Winchester Assumes Command of the Army—Harrison Directs Clearing of Roads and Building of Forts Barbee, Jennings, and Amanda—Winchester Marches Army from Fort Wayne to Defiance—British Force Checked on their Way to Fort Wayne—Harrison Reappointed Chief in Command of Northwestern Army—Visits Winchester at Defiance and Settles Discord—Plans Fort Winchester, which Was Built at Defiance—Extreme Sufferings of Winchester's Left Wing of the Army—Battle of Mississinewa River.

CHAPTER XIX

THE SECOND GREAT DISASTER OF THE WAR OF 1812 222

Advance of General Winchester's Army from Defiance—Safe Arrival at Presque Isle below

Roche de Bout—There Builds Fort Deposit—Unwise Advance of Army to the Raisin—Defeat and Massacre—Harrison Gathers a New Army and Takes Command—Fort Deposit Abandoned—Fort Winchester again the Frontier Post—Fort Meigs Built—Efforts to Strike the Enemy Unavailing.

CHAPTER XX

A THIRD GREAT DISASTER IN THE FIRST YEAR OF THE WAR 233

The Northwestern Army Neglected by the General Government—General Harrison not Distracted by Unwise Advisers—Investment and Siege of Fort Meigs—Reinforcements for the Fort Disobey Orders—They Are Surrounded and Captured—Further Massacre and Cannibalism by British Allies—The Enemy Raises Siege and Retreats.

CHAPTER XXI

SECOND GREAT EFFORT OF THE ENEMY UNAVAILING 244

The British Gather More Savage Allies—More Preparations by Americans for Advancing upon the Enemy—Celebration of Fourth of July by Soldiers in the Forest—The Enemy Becoming More Active—Fort Seneca Built to Retain Friendship of Aged Aborigines—Second Investment of Fort Meigs by Increased Force—Scheme for its Capture Unavailing—Second Retreat of Enemy from Fort Meigs.

CHAPTER XXII

ANOTHER SIGNAL REPULSE OF THE ALLIED ENEMY 256

British Surround and Attack Fort Stephenson—They are Brilliantly Repulsed by Captain Croghan—They again Retreat to Fort Malden.

CHAPTER XXIII

THE ENTIRE FORCE OF THE BRITISH ON LAKE ERIE CAPTURED 262

Renewed Efforts for Squadron of Armed Vessels Successful—Oliver H. Perry Builder and Commander—His Difficulties—He Sails for the Enemy—Communicates with Harrison—Meets and Captures All of the British Squadron—Perry's Despatches after the Battle—The Killed and Wounded—Description of Squadrons.

CHAPTER XXIV

THE AMERICANS SEEK THE BRITISH AT FORT MALDEN 275

Definite Preparations for the Invasion of Canada—Observance of the Day of Fasting and Prayer—A Sham Battle—Enthusiastic Enlisting in Kentucky for the Invasion—Aged Aborigine Warriors Join the Ranks—The Crossing of Lake Erie—Arrival at Fort Malden—Found Deserted and Fired by the Enemy.

CHAPTER XXV

THE BRITISH PURSUED AND CAPTURED AT THE THAMES 284

Pursuit of the British through Canada—Detroit Recovered by Americans, who Hasten to Complete Victory at the Thames—Aborigines Desert their Allies and Flock to the Americans—General Cass Appointed Military and Civil Governor of Michigan Territory—Name of Detroit's Fort Changed to that of Shelby—Kentucky Troops Return Home by Way of the Raisin.

Contents

CHAPTER XXVI

THE OHIO COUNTRY FREE FROM THE SAVAGE
ALLIANCE 292

Proctor's Request and Harrison's Reply—Harrison Goes to Reinforce Army of the Centre—Period of Quiet in the Ohio Country—General Harrison Resigns—Renewed Efforts for Defence and Advance—Scarcity of Food and Money—Further Neglect by Eastern Authorities—Expeditions through Canada—Unfortunate Expedition to the North.

CHAPTER XXVII

SUCCESS OF THE WAR FOR INDEPENDENCE
ASSURED 303

The Treaty of Ghent Closing the War of 1812–14—Further Confirmation of American Claim of Notorious Methods by the British.

INDEX 311

The Ohio Country
Between the Years 1783 and 1815

The Ohio Country

CHAPTER I

INTRODUCTION

The Settling of the British and French in America—Their Inebriation of the Aborigines—Made them Savages Indeed—Habitual Contention for Ascendancy—Success of the British with the Savages, and against the French—Use of Savages against Colonists during Revolutionary War by the British the Same as against the French in Previous Years.

FRENCHMEN, early in the seventeenth century, were the first Europeans to explore the American country about the Great Lakes and the upper Mississippi River. The course of their travel at first, and for many years after, was up the St. Lawrence River to Montreal, thence up the Ottawa River to Mattawa, thence along the outlet and through the Lakes Talon and Trout, thence by portage to Lake Nipissing, through it and down its outlet the French River into Georgian Bay, and thence southward and westward.

The British[1] ranged along the Atlantic coast south of the St. Lawrence Gulf. They did not abandon their quarrels with the French on leaving England; in fact they added to the old, a new grievance against the French because of the latter's settlement in the new country which the British claimed by "the right of discovery," though this discovery was only a part of the Atlantic shore line.

During the one hundred and fifty years following the coming of the French, quarrels and wars raged in America and elsewhere between these two peoples. Here the French had the advantage for several generations, owing to their early explorations, their maps, and their early free association with and amiable treatment of the Aborigines. Their first, and principal, association was with the Algonquins and the Huron (Wyandot) tribe, both of whom were often at war with the Iroquois of New York. The latter controlled the country south of the course of the French, and southward from Lake Erie and thence westward even to the

[1] The term British is here used to designate the combined force of English, Irish, Scotch, and other Europeans who, at different times, acted with them.

Mississippi River. For a long time this condition had much to do with keeping the French to the northward.

The skins of fur-bearing animals were the principal gain derived by the French, first the *coureurs des bois* particularly; and they gratified in addition their love of adventure and of free life among the Aborigines, which life the roaming French sought later to make free also from the taxes of the Church and the government. Instead of endeavoring to elevate the Aborigines to their degree of civilization, many of them descended to the level of the Aborigines.

As for the Aborigines, the Frenchmen's brandy was to them a revelation. At first merely a pleasing and exhilarating beverage, this soon became a necessity in increasing quantity; a drink which, with them as with countless multitudes before and since, civilized according to their times and associations, was in their more sober moments considered the bane of their lives. It was a drink which held them in abject slavery and was obtained at any cost; for its use had developed in them a thirst for it that outvalued and overbalanced every other consideration. The Frenchmen in trading had also given them knives of steel to replace the clumsy, flint knives of native workmanship; also metal tomahawks, and, later, flint-lock muskets; with which weapons, when elated with the brandy, they felt more than equal to the French themselves. These weapons, with the brandy, made them Savages indeed; the fiercest and most dangerous known to history.

The British, also, became strong competitors of the French; the government for the taxes and the traders for their profits in the fur trade among the Aborigines. At first they dealt with the Algonquins of New England and the Iroquois of New York. Then the Algonquins and the Huron (Wyandot) tribe of the West were invited, by agents, who distributed among them strong drink and gaudy presents, to visit the chief executive in New York. Nothing pleased the Aborigine chiefs more, while resting from war, than to journey hundreds of miles for such a visit, as they were sure of being fed to satiety, and fully loaded with presents for the return; and the new bidder, therefore, was given the preference in their estimation, for there was always a prospect of better terms with him than those received from the former dealer.

The impassive manners and "heavier drinks" of the Englishmen did not, in the estimation of the Aborigines, displace the more affable Frenchmen with their brandy until, by degrees, the British general government showed its power and its attractions, by its armies, by the new products of its looms, and by the larger number and the improved versatility of its traders among the larger tribes. Not until the year 1760 did the British succeed the French government in America.

During all these many generations of intrigue and war between the British and French, the Aborigines and their descendants (all of whom will continue to be here designated Aborigines or Savages, the term "Indian" being an ancient misnomer that should not be perpetuated) were tutored in intrigue and savagery; and they were apt pupils in everything seen among their tutors that was worse than that to which they had been addicted.

For an untold number of generations the Savages had been reared to war with other tribes, and it was inculcated in them that their highest ambition should be to inflict the greatest injury possible upon every individual and tribe they might think worth exploiting for any cause, or for no cause. The intoxicating beverages and modern weapons received from their new tutors made them good allies in the eyes of these tutors. The

British and the French vied with each other in bidding intoxicating beverages, weapons, and other things desired by them, each for the purpose of winning the trade and the warrior support of the Savages against the other.

The French sent missionaries and traders among the Iroquois; but with great effort the British succeeded in retaining most of the trade of these "Six Nations" and their good will. Had the French succeeded in their efforts with this strong confederacy, the final result of their contention with the British would have been delayed, if not altogether different.

In the year 1747, the British succeeded in causing a conspiracy of Chief Nicholas and the Hurons (Wyandots) against the French; but the latter soon regained the friendship of this strong tribe.

Scalps of both British and French, taken by the Savages, were purchased by both respectively; a most inhuman bidding for the lives of each other that reacted disastrously upon both. For a time the Savages could get scalps either way they roamed; and at times neither purchaser could feel sure he was not buying scalps taken from his own countrymen.

The Savages, themselves as low in the scale of humanity as it seemed possible to descend, were

Introduction

often cloyed, wearied to satiety, by the unceasing intrigue and bloodshed between the Europeans, which had been going on in America for fully five generations.

But the British have ever been noted for their persistency as well as for their aggressiveness, and the final victory over the French in America was theirs in the year 1760, in which year the French forts at Detroit and elsewhere were peacefully surrendered to them.

The troubles of the British with the western tribes of Savages, however, did not end with the acquisition of the fort at Detroit, and the fort at the head of the Maumee River; which forts had been the centres of many merry entertainments of the Savages, and had witnessed the equipping of war parties by the French against the British. The Savages had not yet witnessed enough of the power and resources of the British to fully understand why they should not continue with the French, or set up war against the British themselves.

Then came the Conspiracy of Pontiac, with which the British had to deal at a great expense of life and money. Much diplomacy was needed also before they were at all comfortable in the hope of securing the Savages as allies in war, which had been their policy from the first. At different times later, they had a great fear that there would be a federation of all the largest northern and southern tribes against them. As late as February 18, 1771, Sir William Johnson, their greatest Aborigine agent, wrote to the British Secretary of State in part as follows:

"It is really a matter of the most serious nature, for if a verry small part of those people have been capable of reducing us to such straits as we were in a few years since, what may we not expect from such a formidable alliance as we are threatened with, when at the same time it is known that we are not at this time more capable of defiance, if so much, as at the former period. This is in some measure the consequence of their becoming better acquainted with their own strength and united capacity to preserve their importance & check our advances into their country."

With the allaying of this fear, came a new opposition to the British government in America, from the British colonists themselves; and, as the opposition to the impositions on the colonists increased, the London and local governments felt more and more the desire, and apparent necessity, for greater efforts to ally the Savages firmly to them, and against the colonists. Surely a strong and even savage alliance was being formed to compel subjection of the colonists, and to yet further impoverish those who had already been impoverished beyond a reasonable limit by the mother country in her wars to overcome the French.

At this late day, at least, the British government should have recognized the full worth of the character of the Pilgrims and Puritans; the value of the conscience that drove them into the distant wilderness one hundred and fifty years before, which conscience, with renewed and renewing love of freedom, had been transmitted to their descendants through the generations, and had been imparted to thousands of Great Britain's hardy, good citizens who, during these many years, had followed their countrymen into this new country. It has been many times shown that the British government had seldom, if ever, taken thought of such sentiment, and proper action regarding it.

Those in authority during this period of time, and later, for forty years at least, were not actuated by humanitarian motives, but by a selfish desire to compel those of the blood of their own countrymen—who had been born and reared in the atmosphere of self-sustaining, if not full, freedom—to absolute obedience to force, wholly regardless of the consequences to the colonists. Could any government have been more thoughtless, even outrageous, in the treatment of its subjects? Could any self-respecting people longer consent to live under such a government? These were the questions uppermost in the minds of the colonists.

It is the office of this Introduction to briefly sketch part of the action of the British authorities in further tutoring the Aborigines in savagery, and more firmly allying them to their efforts to conquer the colonists during the Revolutionary War, as somewhat of a preparation and perspective for what follows.

Detroit was the principal western post of the French, and it became such to the British immediately after their conquest of the French.

When the Revolutionary War seemed imminent, the office of Lieutenant-Governor and Superintendent of Indian Affairs was created for the western country, with headquarters at Detroit. Captain, afterwards Colonel, Henry Hamilton of the 15th Regiment of British troops was appointed to this office. Arriving at Detroit November 9, 1775, he assumed the duties required of him. He proved tactful toward the Savages, cruel and remorseless toward the Colonists.

Previous to this date "war belts" had been sent out from Detroit to the different tribes for their meetings in council; and such "councils" had been

Introduction

held, in which rum flowed freely, its insidious effects being supplemented by every incitement calculated to inflame the Savages against the Amercans "who were endeavoring to crowd them from their lands, and now had rebelled against the good king, their father, who was distributing so many presents and kindnesses to his Indian children." Early in September, 1776, the new officer, Hamilton, wrote to Lord George Germain, his superior in office, that "The Ottawas, Chippewas, Wyandottes and Pottawatomies, with the Senecas would fall on the scattered settlers on the Ohio and its branches . . . whose arrogance, disloyalty and imprudence has justly drawn upon them this deplorable sort of war."

Lord Germain took pleasure in employing agents who would incite the Savages of the wilderness to "fall on the Americans." He had complained of Sir Guy Carleton, afterwards Lord Dorchester, Governor of Canada, for not making full use of the Savages; and Carleton later acquiesced in this inhuman work. Carleton wrote to Hamilton, October 6, 1776, to "Keep the Indians in readiness to join me in the Spring, or march elsewhere as they may be most wanted."

War parties of Savages, thoroughly equipped, and commanded by British officers, were sent out from Detroit, east, south, and to the southwest, wherever they could find the most defenceless American settlements in Ohio, Pennsylvania, Virginia, and Kentucky, to plunder and to kill. Places of refuge were attacked and, if the protectors could be overcome, all the wounded and feeble were massacred and the others taken captive, perhaps to suffer a more painful death. Governor Hamilton reported to Secretary Germain under date July 27, 1777, that he had sent out fifteen war parties composed of two hundred and eighty-nine Savage warriors with thirty British officers and rangers. He reported to Governor Carleton January 15, 1778, that: "The parties sent from hence have been generally successful, although the Indians have lost men enough to sharpen their resentment; they have brought in 23 prisoners alive, twenty of which they presented to me, and 129 scalps."

Occasionally a war party would number several hundred, but usually they were much smaller, viz.: August 25, 1778, fifteen Miamis were started; September 5th, thirty-one Miamis; September 9th, one Frenchman, five Chippewas, and fifteen Miamis, are the statements of a few of the individual reports. Hamilton reported September 16th that his parties "had taken thirty-four prisoners, seventeen of which they delivered up, and eighty-one scalps."

All scalps were paid for. When the Savages started out on their raids, the Governor, and sometimes the commandant of the post also, encouraged them by singing the war song, by the gift of some weapon, or by passing the weapons of the Savages through their own hands, by this act "taking hold of the same tomahawk" to show full sympathy in the murderous work. On their return to Detroit the Savages were sometimes welcomed by the firing of the fort's cannon. Hamilton was charged with having stated prices for American scalps, but generally none for prisoners.

The flow of rum was so great in Detroit, and the activity of the Savages was so much impaired thereby, that an official inquiry was instituted by Governor Haldimand. Only active persons were wanted; and the British organization and discipline pervaded every quarter.

Governor William Tryon of New York wrote to Secretary Germain in London, under date July 28, 1779, that: "My opinions remain unchangeable respecting the utility of depradatory excursions. I think Rebellion must soon totter if those excursions are reiterated and made to extremity."

Captain Lernoult at Detroit did not prove himself equal to the demands of his more cruel superiors, and he was superseded in October by Major Arent Schuyler De Peyster, a pronounced loyalist from New York.

Efforts were renewed to establish more effective war parties of Savages. Some scalps had been brought in, but the letters of the new commandant to Governor Haldimand under date of October 20th and November 20th show disgust at the great quantities of rum drunk by the Savages; and also at their inefficiency, for the Savages feared to make any more effective raids owing to their dread of American retaliation.

The successes of the Americans, aided by some Frenchmen, at Vincennes and at the Illinois posts under command of the patriotic, brave, and intrepid Colonel George Rogers Clark, one of which entailed the capture of the notorious Lieutenant-Governor Hamilton, with his command and supplies, induced many American families to move from the East in the autumn of 1779; and during the next spring three hundred family boats arrived at the falls of the Ohio River, near the present city of Louisville, Kentucky, with immigrants from the East.

The Savages were generally more inactive during the cold weather; but they were started out

Introduction 15

early in the spring. Colonel De Peyster reported May 16, 1780, that:

"The prisoners daily brought in here [Detroit] are part of the thousand families who are flying from the oppression of Congress in order to add to the number already settled in Kentuck, the finest country for new settlers in America; but it happens, unfortunately for them, to be the best hunting ground of the Indians which they will never give up and, in fact, it is our interest not to let the Virginians, Marylanders, and Pennsylvanians get possession there, lest, in a short time, they become formidable to this post."

May 26th De Peyster wrote to Captain Patt. Sinclair, who had been named Lieutenant-Governor and Superintendent of Indian Affairs at Michilimackinac (now called Mackinac) for the more northern district, that: "Everything is quiet here except the constant noise of the war drum. All the Seiginies [Saginaw Aborigines] are arrived at the instance of the Shawnees and Delawares. More Indians from all quarters than ever known before, and not a drop of rum!"

June 1st, De Peyster wrote to Governor Haldimand that he had already fitted out two thousand warriors and sent them along the Ohio and Wabash rivers; and the returns were hundreds of scalps and prisoners.

Various plans were made by the Americans for

the capture of Detroit, but sufficient military force could not be gathered. Appeals were made to General Washington, who fully appreciated the necessity for decided action in this direction, but he replied:

"It is out of my power to send any reinforcements to the westward. If the States would fill their Continental battalions, we would be able to oppose a regular and permanent force to the enemy in every quarter. If they will not, they must certainly take measures to defend themselves by their militia, however expensive and ruinous the system."

The various claims of the Eastern Colonies to the territory west of the Allegheny Mountains, based on old English charters, had been the cause of friction between these Colonies for many years, and it required yet more time to adjust properly this and similar affairs to the Colonies' mutual advantage.

Continued attacks of the Savages on the frontier, resulting in great loss of life to the Americans, including the defeat of militia and volunteers sent against the marauders, caused fresh and increased terror among all the frontier settlements. Thomas Jefferson, then Governor of Virginia, appealed to General Washington for aid and received reply, written at New Windsor December 28, 1781, that:

Introduction

"I have ever been of the opinion that the reduction of the post of Detroit would be the only certain means of giving peace and security to the whole western frontier, and I have constantly kept my eyes upon that object; but such has been the reduced state of our Continental force, and such the low ebb of our funds, especially of late, that I have never had it in my power to make the attempt."

Other attempts by the Colonies, and settlers in the West, to reduce the British post at Detroit reacted unfavorably upon those making them, from their want of a sufficient number of well disciplined men. Nor could the frontier settlements with their refuge blockhouses be well protected against the great number of thoroughly organized British forces, principally Savages, which were continually being sent out from Detroit up to the close of the Revolutionary War. Even when attained, the desired peace was of short duration, as will be told in the following pages.

CHAPTER II

BRITISH DIRECT NON-OBSERVANCE OF TREATY OF PARIS, AND THEN SIGN THE TREATY

The First Years Following the Revolutionary War—The First Northwestern Boundary Line—The Aborigines Willing to be Friends of the United States—Causes of their Alliance with the British—The British Continue to Hold Military Posts in Opposition to Treaty—Large Amount of American Property Purloined by the British.

THE Treaty of Paris closing the Revolutionary War was signed at Versailles September 3, 1783, about ten months after the preliminary agreement which stopped hostilities. This treaty distinctly set forth that the territory south from the middle of the Great Lakes and their connecting waters, and east from the middle of the upper Mississippi River, should belong to the United States, and that Great Britain should "with all convenient speed" withdraw her troops and belongings from Detroit and other parts of this territory.

From 1783-1791

The American Aborigines were willing, as they had been in 1760 at the time of the British succession to the territories of the French, to befriend the nation which gave them presents most munificently and which most freely indulged their sensualities accordingly. In May, 1783, Benjamin Lincoln, the American Secretary of War, sent Ephraim Douglas to the Aborigines of Ohio, and farther west, to encourage, and win, their friendship to the United States, they having been "allies" of the British during the war, and not inclined to stop hostilities in compliance with the agreement.

Douglas arrived at Sandusky, Ohio, the 7th of June and passed some days in that place with the Delaware Aborigines; he then went among the Wyandots, Ottawas, and Miamis along the lower Maumee River. On July 4th he arrived at Detroit, and there Colonel De Peyster, British commandant of the post, called a council, ostensibly in the American agent's favor, at which the following tribes were represented, viz.: Chippewa, Delaware, Kickapoo, Miami, Ottawa, "Oweochtanos," Piankishaw, Pottawotami, Seneca, Shawnee, and Wyandot. Mr. Douglas reported:

"Most of them gave evident marks of their satisfaction at seeing a subject of the United States in the country. They carried their civilities so far that my lodging was all day surrounded with crowds of them when at home, and the streets lined with them to attend my going abroad, that they might have an opportunity of seeing and saluting me, which they did not fail to do in their best manner with every demonstration of joy."

Mr. Douglas returned to Niagara on July 11th and his further reports lead to the inference that he did not comprehend the full cause of the adherence of the Savages to the British during the war, or the mercenary cause of their dogging his steps during his visit among them; and that he had no foreboding of the many bloody years that were to follow.

The British allowances to the Aborigines had largely ceased when the agreement preliminary to the treaty was signed. The Savage "allies" were therefore short of rum and provisions; and they hoped to receive from the agent of the conquering nation fresh and more liberal supplies.[1]

[1] The cause of the popularity and continued successes of the British with the Aborigines is plain, and to the discredit of both parties. They outbid the French, and the Americans, in their lavish giving of intoxicants and articles that delighted the palates and eyes of the Savages; and exceeded other nations in the general, and special, aid extended the Savages for the free indulgence of their bloodthirsty natures enhanced by strong drink. The British expenditures for this purpose during the Revolutionary War grew apace, and in the view

The British government was fully apprised of the difficulties, and the improper aggressiveness, of its conduct toward and with the American Aborigines, before and after the close of the war. Colonel De Peyster early saw the danger of the course prescribed for him, and he wrote to Governor Haldimand accordingly.

Also, immediately after the preliminary treaty of Paris, the British began to experience the embarrassment of their desired relation to the Aborigines,—of the difficulties in retaining their full influence over them while lessening expenditures for them. Colonel De Peyster reported from Detroit to Governor Haldimand's secretary June 18, 1783, before the arrival there of the American agent, Ephraim Douglas, that:

"We are all in expectation of news. Everything that is bad is spread through the Indian country but,

---

of the central office the amounts became "enormous and amazing," aggregating millions of dollars. From December 25, 1777, to August 31, 1778, there were received at Detroit 371,460 barrels of flour; 42,176 lbs. fresh beef; 16,473 lbs. salt beef; 203,932 lbs. salt pork; 19,756 lbs. butter; and great quantities of mutton, corn, peas, oatmeal, rice, and rum. In the summer of 1778 fifty-eight and a half tons of gunpowder were sent to Detroit from Niagara, of which the Savages received the largest share, as there were in Detroit August 30, 1778, but four hundred and eighty-two militiamen with little use for ammunition in or near the fort. For additional statements, *see* Zeisberger's *Diary*, and Slocum's *History of the Maumee River Basin*.

as I have nothing more than the King's proclamation from authority, I evade answering impertinent questions. Heavens! if goods do not arrive soon, what will become of me? I have lost several stone weight of flesh within these twenty days. I hope Sir John [Johnson, British Superintendent of Indian Affairs] is to make us a visit."

To prevent complications, and consequent quarrels, the United States Congress, in 1783, forbade the purchase of land from the Aborigines by individuals or companies. The British, however, continued their machinations with these Aborigines.

Agent Ephraim Douglas reported February 2, 1784, that early in the fall of 1783, Sir John Johnson assembled the different western tribes of Aborigines on United States soil, at Sandusky, Ohio, and having prepared them with lavish distribution of presents, addressed them in part as follows, Simon Girty being their interpreter, viz.:

"The King, his and their common father, had made peace with the Americans, and had given them the land possessed by the British on this continent; but the report of his having given them any part of their [the Aborigines'] lands was false, and fabricated by the Americans for the purpose of provoking them against their father; that they should, therefore, shut their eyes against it. So far the contrary was proved, that the great River Ohio was to be the line between the Indians in this quarter and the Americans, over

From 1783-1791

which the latter ought not to pass and return in safety."

It had become evident, in other ways, also, that the British, although defeated in war, yet had ulterior designs against the young Republic. The definitive Treaty of Paris reads in part that:

"His Britannic Majesty shall with all convenient speed, and without causing any destruction, or carrying away any negroes or other property of the American inhabitants, withdraw all his armies, garrisons, and fleets from the said United States, and from every post, place, and harbor within the same."

The British had not complied with this agreement nor made any effort to do so at nine or more posts, viz.: Point au Fer and Dutchman's Point, by Lake Champlain; Oswegatchie near the present Ogdensburg, New York; Oswego, Niagara, Fort Erie, Sandusky, Detroit, Michilimackinac, and perhaps one or two more small places; Detroit being the principal post of all for their purpose.

General Washington had not been pleased with the trend of affairs. In the interest of peace with the British, and between the frontier settlements and Aborigines, he sent Baron von Steuben of the United States Army to Governor Haldimand of Canada, July 12, 1783, to ask that orders be issued for the withdrawal of the British troops from

Detroit and other posts in American territory, whence they persisted in dominating the Aborigines throughout Ohio and the Southwest. The reply was that no orders had been received from his superior for such withdrawal. Governor Clinton was refused the surrender of the posts in New York May 10, 1784, as was Governor Chittenden of Vermont, the posts in his State by Lake Champlain. Haldimand afterward wrote that these demands by States were easily answered; "the Treaty being with Congress, a post could not be surrendered to a State"; a point well taken.

A formal demand for the surrender of these posts was sent by General Knox, Secretary of War, by messenger Lieutenant-Colonel William Hull, July 12, 1784. Again Haldimand's reply was that he had received no orders to evacuate the posts, which, while truthful in a sense, was a dissimulation, as he had received orders not to evacuate them; and, under the circumstances, he should have had honor enough to so state.

The Treaty of Paris was ratified by Congress January 14, 1784, and by Great Britain April 9, 1784. The British ministry had decided before this time to hold the posts, and the Secretary so notified Haldimand in a letter which was dated the day before the ratification. Here was perfidy and duplicity in keeping with many other orders from Great Britain and with acts of her agents in America, both before and after this date.

No one could be found to give tangible explanation or reason for the non-compliance with the treaty. How different this from the last injunction of Lord Chatham, in his reply to the Duke of Richmond, who, when the British cause in America was tottering, said, "if we must fall, let us fall like men!"

In her supreme arrogance, Great Britain disdained sending a minister to the United States. John Adams, however, was sent to England in 1785 as Minister or Agent, but was received generally with indifference. Writes one of England's historians:

"The King, who had previously declared to some of his attendants that he looked forward to his first interview with this new minister as the most critical moment of his life, received him very graciously, and said to him, with that honest candor which was a conspicuous part of his character, 'I was the last man in the kingdom, sir, to consent to the independence of America; but, now it is granted, I shall be the last man in the kingdom to sanction a violation of it.'"

We read further:

"The King, on coming to the crown, had supposed that he had nothing to do but to study the welfare of his people; but he soon found that he had also to study the tempers and jealousies of his ministers, who, though they were his ostensible servants, were, in fact, his masters."

This was not the condition of affairs evident in the year 1775, from which time his Majesty's officers in America complied literally, and liberally, with his injunction to Lord Dunmore, Governor of Virginia, "to arm the negroes and Indians"; and, also, with his positive orders to Guy Johnson, agent among the Six Nations of Iroquois in New York: "to secure their assistance, to . . . Lose no time; induce them to take up the hatchet against his Majesty's rebellious subjects in America. It is a service of very great importance; fail not to exert every effort that may tend to accomplish it; use the utmost diligence and activity."

This was the keynote to one of the most unholy and inhuman alliances known to history. Fail not to exert every effort that may tend to accomplish the alliance of the American Savages, the worst in history, with the British, was the British slogan throughout the Revolutionary War and for many years thereafter, particularly in the old Northwestern, and Southwestern, Territories.

The conscientious General Washington suggested, December 14, 1784, that possibly the nonpayment of individual debts to British subjects might be a reason (he did not say a valid one) for the British retention of American posts; and the British slowly got hold of this idea. Minister Adams, during his efforts in London to get some satisfaction for their non-compliance with agreement, could only get an occasional hint about debts. The Marquis of Carmarthen, being pressed by Adams, was led to state that the posts would not be delivered until the debts were paid. Adams warmly replied that such payment was not stipulated in the treaty; and that no government undertook to pay the private debts of its subjects. Adams could do no more, in fact nothing, to get what he considered a respectful hearing and proper treatment of this or of other questions relating to the best interests of the two countries, or to the United States, and he returned home.

While showing no favor to the United States the British desired to have an official representative in the country that they might be kept informed regarding the sentiments and acts of the people, and of the government. For this purpose, Sir John Temple was appointed consul in November, 1785, and, upon discussion of the matter, he was received by the State Department as a favor to Great Britain.

In December, 1786, Phineas Bond was sent to London as consul to Great Britain from New York, Pennsylvania, Delaware, and Maryland. After a period of hesitancy on the part of the government, he was received; and in later years it was acknowledged by the British that Mr. Bond was of service to them, and no complaints were made by the States that sent him.

The United States government instituted inquiries regarding the laws of the several States against the collection of debts by foreigners; and some such laws that might prove obnoxious to some subjects of Great Britain were repealed.[1]

Early in 1791, Thomas Jefferson, Secretary of State, sent Gouverneur Morris to London as private agent, to learn the sentiment of the British ministry regarding: "1st, Their retention of the American military posts; 2nd, Indemnification for the Negroes carried away by the British soldiers; 3rd, A treaty for the regulation of commerce, and 4th, The exchange of ministers."

Morris, from his more affable nature and his

[1] In this connection, *see* Benjamin Franklin's articles on *Sending Felons to America*, and his *Retort Courteous* for sarcasm regarding the British desire to be paid by the people whose property they had destroyed after the treaty, either personally or at any rate through their allies. Also compare the *Laws of Virginia* regarding claims; and several letters of Henry Knox, Secretary of War, No. 150, Volume i.

From 1783-1791

greater love for high society, also probably from his more facile business training, dwelt much nearer the governing forces in London than did Adams; and his powers of observation, and discernment, were none the less clear. He felt obliged to report that the British

"were decided not to surrender the posts in any event; and as our courts were shut against the collection of debts, they suggested indemnification on our part, and that they would set it so high (if it was admitted) as to insure disagreement; that they had measures for concealing the Negroes carried away; and lastly, that they equivocated on every proposal of a treaty of commerce."

Here, at last, was somewhat of a statement, gathered piecemeal and informally, showing that the British, as usual, continued to arrogate to themselves the right to treat the United States disrespectfully, according only to their supreme selfishness, regardless of the formal treaty!

A recent English writer says[1]:

"Considering the clouded state of the political horizon, it is not surprising that Morris's patience was tried by an unwillingness of the British ministers to commit themselves to any arrangement with him. As statesmen of the Old World, they could condone

[1] Edward Smith, in his *England and America after Independence*, page 23.

the irregularity of his secret mission. But it was their business to temporize, and see what turn European affairs would take."

This confession of selfish arrogance was probably the truth of the matter. They had the advantage over the young Republic, and were determined to keep it, while alleging the complexity of European troubles as an excuse.

Not a word was at this time uttered regarding improper treatment of their friends, the Tories, many of whom remained even after the withdrawal of the British armies, and for whom the tender conscience of some American statesmen had awakened some sympathy in the States. It is probably true that in some parts of the States the treatment of loyalists (Tories) did not fully accord with the phrasing of the Treaty of Paris on this subject; though it did accord with right and reason. There had been many instances of extreme violence during the war by these loyalists against the hard-pressed colonists; instances where they had taken up arms and led the British against their neighbors, and otherwise clandestinely caused the death of neighbors on account of their efforts for independence; and it was beyond reason that such persons (Tories) would be welcomed as though they had the full rights of patriots, or even tolerated in such neighborhoods after the close of the war. The Americans quite agreed that all such persons should have departed with the British. For them to remain on or near the scenes of so much suffering and bloodshed, as constant reminders of their participation in the cause of it, was but to invite the punishment they fully deserved.

In August, 1791, Great Britain sent her first Minister, George Hammond, to the United States. He was well received; and President Washington soon appointed Thomas Pinckney Minister to Great Britain. Secretary Jefferson, in his direct way, soon approached Hammond regarding the continued occupancy of American military posts by British troops, and requested their withdrawal. "Being pressed as to the full extent of his powers," Hammond acknowledged that he was not empowered to perform any definite act or agreement, and that his instructions were of a general "plenipotentiary" character.

President Washington's proclamation of neutrality between the French and British in another of their quarrels, and his later letter to the French expressing general confidence, together with the requested recall of the French Minister by the United States government, displeased the parties at home and abroad, as is usual in such cases.

The British plot was deepening. For her increasing European war expenditures, she was receiving great profits from her continued deprivation of the United States of the American Aborigine trade. By retaining the United States' posts, she could continue to dominate the Aborigines and the western country in its trade, and possibly in its destiny.

CHAPTER III

DEVELOPMENT OF THE WEST CHECKED BY BRITISH INFLUENCES

Aborigine Claims to Land Based on Conquest, which Claims the Savages and the British Were not Willing to Accede to the United States, their Conqueror—Treaties with Aborigines—Reservations—Cession to United States of Western Claims by States—Civil Organizations—Surveys for Settlements—Ohio Land Companies—Fort Finney Built—Continued Control of Aborigines by British—Expeditions against Savage Marauders—Desire in the West for Independence from the United States—Unauthorized Retaliations on Spaniards Allayed.

THE Aborigines continued to be unsettled and to threaten the peace; and the United States government continued a pacific policy toward them and the British.

The Legislature of New York for some time after the Treaty of Paris favored the expulsion from American territory of the Six Nations (the Iroquois of New York), on account of their instability and treachery; but this question was finally settled by the United States Congress in favor of continued forbearance, and it was decided that efforts be made to keep them as fully as possible from British influence; to civilize them by treaty, and to confine them to narrower limits by gradually and nominally purchasing their claims to territory unnecessary to them.

Accordingly, October 22, 1784, a treaty was effected at Fort Stanwix, on the site of the present city of Rome, New York, where the Six Nations relinquished all claims to the country west of the Allegheny Mountains. These claims were based on the idea, shared alike by them and the British, that they were entitled to this territory by virtue of their conquest of the western tribes; but they did not want to accord the Americans a similar right to this territory, which the Americans had wrested from these Savages, as well as from the British, by hard-won victories.

Virginia ceded to the United States all of her right, title, and claim, derived by charter from Queen Elizabeth, to the country northwest of the Ohio River, March 1, 1784. Congress was prepared for this act, and by a committee, of which Thomas Jefferson was chairman, reported the same day a plan for its temporary government. The names proposed for the divisions of this territory not meeting with approval by Congress, they were erased from the plan April 23d; and later this suggested plan for division was rejected.

Continuing its humane policy toward the Aborigines, the United States, by Commissioners George Rogers Clark, Richard Butler, and Arthur Lee, met the chiefs of the Chippewa, Delaware, Ottawa, and Wyandot tribes at Fort McIntosh, on the right bank of the Ohio River at the mouth of Beaver Creek about twenty-nine miles below Pittsburg, and January 21, 1785, effected a treaty in which the limits of their territory were agreed upon as follows: the Maumee River on the west, and the Cuyahoga on the east; from Lake Erie to a line running westward from Fort Laurens, by the Tuscarawas River, to the portage on the headwaters of the Miami River, at Loramie; all being in the present State of Ohio. Reservations were made by the United States of tracts six miles square, at this portage, at the mouth of the Maumee River, and two miles square at the lower Sandusky River. Three Aborigine chiefs were to remain hostages with the Commissioners until all American prisoners then held by the Aborigines were surrendered.

Overtures for treaty and peace were also made to the Miami, Pottawotami, Piankishaw, and other western tribes, but, through the influence of the British and French with whom they associated, and who were in opposition to the American system of government, land surveys, and definite land titles, the desired treaty could not be effected. A large council of these tribes, however, was held, the following August, at Ouiotenon, generally known as Wea, by the Wabash River, where the policy of continuing savage raids on American frontier settlements was inculcated.

On April 19, 1785, the Legislature of Massachusetts released to the general government her claims in the Northwestern Territory, excepting a small part in southeastern Michigan which was released May 30, 1800. This claim, like other claims by the Colonies, was based on the old English charters, or patents, the English deriving their right from their discovery of the Atlantic shore.

The desire of the immigrants from the Eastern States to obtain western lands for settlement became so great after the treaty of Fort McIntosh, that this, combined with the necessity of establishing permanent lines for titles, induced Congress to pass, on May 20, 1785, "An Ordinance for Ascertaining the Mode of Disposing of Lands in the Western Territory," which provided for

From 1784-1787

the survey and marking of lines of townships, water-power sites, etc.

"Several disorderly persons having crossed the Ohio River and settled upon unappropriated lands," Congress passed an act, June 15, 1785, prohibiting such intrusions, and commanding the intruders "to depart with their families and effects without loss of time, as they shall answer the same at their peril." This action was taken to protect the lives of the would-be settlers, as two members of the four families who settled near the mouth of the Scioto River were killed by Savages in April. The action of Congress was also intended to allay the antipathy of the Savages, while preparing the country for formal settlement. It was during this summer that the extensive purchases of land by the Ohio Company of Associates, and by John Cleves Symmes, were negotiated.

A few United States troops occasionally passed along the Ohio River from Fort Pitt (now Pittsburg) to and from Vincennes and Kaskaskia, escorting officers, carrying despatches, and convoying supplies. October 22, 1785, the building of Fort Finney was begun by Major Finney's command on the bank of the Big Miami River, about a mile above its mouth in the Ohio. Here, on January 31, 1786, commissioners effected a treaty with the

Shawnees, with Wyandot and Delaware representatives as witnesses, wherein land was allotted to them southwest of that allotted at the treaty of Fort McIntosh, and extending to the Wabash River, with like conditions. Hostages were retained for the return of American captives, as at other treaties; but the hostages escaped, and very few captives were returned. The Miamis and other tribes farther west were urged to participate in these treaties, but they again declined, they being more strongly under British influence.[1]

A large number of settlers from the East continued to come into the Ohio River Valley; and depredations on them by the Savages became so frequent and exasperating that a thousand Kentuckians, under command of General Clark, marched to Vincennes against the tribes along the Wabash River in the fall of 1786; but poor supplies and disaffection among the volunteers caused the expedition to return without having punished the enemy.

Nearly eight hundred mounted riflemen under Colonel Benjamin Logan were fitted out against the hostile Shawnees, and, detouring the head-

[1] *See* the United States State Department MSS., No. 56, pages 345, 395, and No. 150. Also the Haldimand Papers during 1784 to 1786.

From 1784-1787

waters of Mad River, in the present Clark and Champaign counties, Ohio, they burned eight large towns of the Aborigines, destroyed many fields of corn, killed about ten warriors including the head chief, and captured thirty-two prisoners.[1]

On September 14, 1786, the State of Connecticut released in favor of the United States her claims to lands in the Northwestern Territory excepting her "Western Reserve" from the forty-first degree of latitude to that of forty-two degrees and two minutes, and from the western line of Pennsylvania to a north and south line one hundred and twenty miles to the west; and that State opened an office for the disposal of that part of the Reserve east of the Cuyahoga River, the eastern boundary of the territory allotted to the Aborigines.

With the increasing population west of the Allegheny Mountains, the free navigation of the Mississippi River became a paramount question; and some misconceptions regarding Secretary John Jay's efforts for a treaty with Spain, combined with the activities of designing men, some of

[1] For full description of the temper of the Savages and of the American settlements, and of efforts of the general government for peace, *see* United States State Department MSS., Nos. 30, 56, 60, and 150. Also the Draper MSS. in the Wisconsin Historical Society Library.

whom were allied to British interests, caused commotion in the Ohio Valley, increasing among the settlements to a clamor for independence, or separation from the American Union. General George R. Clark, whose active command, to curtail expenses, had been withdrawn July 2, 1783, acting with others at Vincennes, decided to garrison the abandoned Post Vincennes. An independent company of men was enlisted early in October, 1786, and, with this company, the goods of Spanish merchants at Vincennes and elsewhere along the Ohio River were seized with a "determination that they should not trade up the river, if they would not let the Americans trade down the Mississippi." The Council of Virginia decided positively against these measures February 28, 1787; and, by resolution of Congress, April 24th, the United States troops along the Ohio River were directed to take immediate and efficient measures "for dispossessing a body of men who had, in a lawless and unauthorized manner, taken possession of Post Vincennes in defiance of the proclamation and authority of the United States." The recently brevetted Brigadier-General Josiah Harmar, with a small force of United States soldiers, then took possession of the post, and allowed Clark and his followers to return to their homes. Thus was averted a possible war with Spain and France combined.

The Americans engaged in these overt acts wrote to their friends that "Great Britain stands ready with open arms to receive and support us. They have already offered to open their resources for our supplies."

CHAPTER IV

CONTINUED NEFARIOUS WORK WITH THE SAVAGES

Activities of the British against the United States—Their Main Fort in American Territory Strengthened—Benedict Arnold with them—Organization of the Territory Northwest of the Ohio River—Increase in Population—Other Civil Organizations—More Systematic Efforts to Check British Influence with American Aborigines—Forts Built—Reports of the Extensive Savage Work Done by the Aborigines—Cannibalism.

THE animus of Great Britain at this time is further shown by a letter of March 22, 1787, from Sir John Johnson to Joseph Brant, the most prominent chief of the Six Nations (Iroquois), regarding the military posts yet held by the British in American territory. This is given in part as follows:

"It is for your [the Aborigines'] sake, chiefly, that we hold them. If you become indifferent about them they may, perhaps, be given up . . . whereas, by supporting them you encourage us to hold them, and discourage the new settlements . . . every day increased by numbers coming in who find they cannot live in the States."

Arthur St. Clair, then Representative in Congress from Pennsylvania, also reported April 13, 1787, the continued infraction of the Treaty of Paris regarding these forts.

The noted Virginia loyalist (Tory) Doctor John Connolly, who had been active against the colonists during the Revolutionary War, and was yet a British subject, resident in Canada, again became active for his king, traversing Ohio and Kentucky in 1787, '88, '89 in efforts to alienate the American settlers from the East, and to ally them with the British for the purpose of capturing the Spanish territory by the lower rivers and controlling the Mississippi Basin. General James Wilkinson charged that Connolly was an emissary direct from Lord Dorchester, then Governor of Canada, and Wilkinson himself was not free from suspicion of being engaged in a similar scheme. The probability of the correctness of Wilkinson's charge against Connolly, however, was strengthened by the fact that, in June of this year, the British garrison at Detroit was largely reinforced from lower Canada, and the next year the fortifications were rebuilt and strengthened by order of Lord Dorchester, who was then there.

These warlike preparations on American territory continued for some length of time, and similar preparations were occasionally made for several years.[1] Benedict Arnold was reported as being in Detroit about June 1, 1790, inspecting the British troops; and on August 25th, President Washington took official notice of the British preparations, which were evidently for a Mississippi campaign.

The Congressional Committee on the Territory Northwest of the Ohio River reported, July 7, 1786, a plan for its division; and the full Ordinance for the government of this Territory was made a law July 13, 1787. This "Ordinance of 1787" marks an era in legislative history. The principal officers for the Northwestern Territory under this Ordinance, who were appointed October 5th, to enter upon their duties February 1, 1788, were the following: Governor, Major-General Arthur St. Clair; Judges, Samuel H. Parsons, James M. Varnum, and John Armstrong; Secretary, Winthrop Sargent. John Armstrong declining to serve,

---

[1] *See* James Wilkinson's *Memoirs*, volume ii; Charles E. A. Gayarre's *History of Louisiana*, volume iii; State Department MSS.; *Virginia State Papers*, volume iv; Draper MSS.; Gardoqui MSS., etc. For accounts of the treachery and savagery of the Aborigines during these years, *see* United States State Department MSS., and Draper MSS.

John Cleves Symmes was appointed to fill the vacancy.

It was estimated that within a year after the organization of this Territory, twenty thousand men, women, and children from the Eastern States passed down the Ohio River to settle in the Ohio River Basin.

The renewal of military preparations by the British in this Territory, centering at Detroit, had an exciting effect upon the American Aborigines, who had long been impatient of their enforced quiet. The increasing settlements in southern Ohio, and south of the river, on lands relinquished by the Aborigines in treaties, and the completion of the organization of the Territory, were eagerly accepted as incentives for repeating their murderous raids upon the settlements.

To allay the maraudings, Congress, July 21, 1787, directed the Superintendent of Aborigine Affairs for the Northern Department, or, if he was unable to attend to it, General Josiah Harmar, to proceed to the most convenient place and make treaty both with the Aborigines of the Wabash River country and with the Shawnees of the central western part of Ohio, and to grant them all assurances consistent with the honor and dignity of the United States.

These and repeated like efforts for peace were unavailing. Thereupon the first instructions by Congress to Governor St. Clair in 1788 were:

1. Examine carefully into the real temper of the Aborigines. 2. Remove if possible all causes of controversy, so that peace and harmony may be established between the United States and the Aborigine tribes. 3. Regulate trade among the Aborigines. 4. Neglect no opportunity that offers for extinguishing the Aborigine claims to lands westward as far as the Mississippi River, and northward as far as the completion of the forty-first degree of north latitude. 5. Use every possible endeavor to ascertain the names of the real head men and warriors of the several tribes, and to attach these men to the United States by every possible proper means. 6. Make every exertion to defeat all confederations and combinations among the tribes; and conciliate the white people inhabiting the frontiers, toward the Aborigines.

The county of Washington in the Northwest Territory was organized in 1778 within the present limits of Ohio; and Governor St. Clair and the judges adopted and published laws, both civil and criminal, for the government and protection of the Territory.

Governor St. Clair succeeded in effecting with the Six Nations another treaty, January 9, 1789, this time at Fort Harmar at the mouth of the Muskingum River by the Ohio; also with the Chippewas, Delawares, Ottawas, Pottawotamis, Sacs, and Wyandots; all of whom confirmed the boundary of Aborigine claims according to previous treaties. These Aborigines at this treaty received from the United States six thousand dollars in money, additional to the payments with former treaties. But a few weeks, however, sufficed to again demonstrate their insincerity, and treachery, their maraudings being resumed with the opening of spring.

General Henry Knox, Secretary of War, reported to President Washington June 13, 1789, that murders by Savages were yet being committed on both sides of the Ohio River, and that the inhabitants were exceedingly alarmed through the extent of six or seven hundred miles; that the settlers had been in constant warfare with the Savages for many years; and that:

"The injuries and murders have been so reciprocal that it would be a point of critical investigation to know on which side they had been the greater. Some of the inhabitants of Kentucky the past year, roused by recent injuries, made an incursion into the Wabash country and, possessing an equal aversion to all bearing the name Indians, they destroyed a number of peaceable Piankishaws who prided themselves in their attachment to the United States. . . . By the best and latest information it appears that by the Wabash and its communications there are from fifteen hundred to two thousand warriors. An expedition with a view of extirpating them, or destroying their towns, could not be undertaken with a probability of success with less than an army of two thousand and five hundred men. The regular troops of the United States on the frontiers are less than six hundred, of which number not more than four hundred could be collected from the posts."

The posts referred to were Forts Pitt, Harmar, Steuben, at the Falls of the Ohio River, and Vincennes.

The Kentuckians again decided to avenge some wrongs they had recently suffered and, on August 26, 1789, Colonel John Hardin led two hundred volunteer cavalrymen across the Ohio River at the Falls, and to the Wabash. They killed six Aborigines, burned one deserted town, and destroyed what corn they found, returning September 28th without the loss of a man.

President Washington addressed Governor St. Clair October 6th desiring full information regarding the Wabash and Illinois Aborigines, and requesting that war with them be averted if possible; but authorizing him to call not more than one thousand militiamen from Virginia and five hundred from Pennsylvania, if necessary, to co-operate with the Federal troops in the Territory. The Governor was also directed to proceed to exe-

From 1787-1790

cute the orders of the late Congress regarding French and other land titles at Vincennes and in the Illinois country, and other matters of organization.

Somewhat later, in the autumn of 1789, Major Doughty's troops built Fort Washington within the site of the present city of Cincinnati, which fort served a useful purpose for several years.

Governor St. Clair and the judges started by boat from Marietta to execute President Washington's instructions about January 1, 1790, and stopped at Fort Washington where they organized the county of Hamilton, and changed the name of the settlement about Fort Washington from that of Losantiville to Cincinnati. Proceeding down the Ohio River, they arrived at Clarksville on January 8th; and thence passed to the Illinois country where they organized St. Clair County, which was to embrace all of the United States' country west of Hamilton County.

To further carry out the President's instructions, a prominent French merchant of Vincennes, Antoine Gamelin, who well understood the temper of the Savages, and by whom he was favorably known, was commissioned by Major Hamtramck to visit and conciliate those Aborigines along the Wabash and Maumee rivers. He started on this mission April 5, 1790; and his report evidenced a desire on the part of the older men of the weaker tribes for peace; but they could not stop their young men, who "were constantly being encouraged and invited to war by the British"; and they were dominated by the stronger tribes, who, in turn, were dominated by the British from whom they received their supplies. All reproached him for coming to them without presents of intoxicants and other supplies. On April 23d, Mr. Gamelin arrived at the Miami towns, at the head of the Maumee River, where the Miamis, Delawares, Pottawotamis, and Shawnees united in telling him they could not give reply to the American overtures for peace until they had consulted the British commandant of the fort at Detroit; they desired, and were given, a copy of the message to them that they might show it to the commandant at Detroit. The British traders in this village were present at the meetings.

Gamelin, being unable to get any satisfaction from the Savages, started on his return from the Miami villages May 2d; and on the 11th reports were received at Vincennes that, three days after his departure, an American captive was roasted and eaten by the Savages at the head of the Maumee River; and that the tribes were sending out war parties in addition to those already operating along the Ohio River.

With hope to check the more active Savages, during the latter half of April, Brigadier-General Josiah Harmar, United States Agent, with one hundred regular troops, seconded by General Charles Scott, with two hundred and thirty Kentucky volunteers, made a detour of the Scioto River, Ohio. They destroyed the food supplies and huts of the hostile Savages but shot only four of them—reporting that "wolves might as well have been pursued."

CHAPTER V

FURTHER CULMINATION OF THE INEFFICIENT MANAGEMENT OF AFFAIRS

Statement of the Conditions by Jurist from Personal Observations—Necessity for Relieving the Long-continued and Severe Sufferings—Kentucky Territory Organized—Other Civil Organizations—General Harmar's Expedition against Hostile Savages at Head of Maumee River—His Army Twice Defeated by them—Their Celebration of Victory at Detroit with their British Allies—Panic along Frontier—The Weak, Inefficient American Conduct of Affairs Reviewed.

EARLY in July, 1790, Judge Henry Inness of Danville, Kentucky, wrote to the Secretary of War, in most part as follows:

"I have been intimately acquainted with this district from 1783, and I can with truth say that in this period the Indians have always been the aggressors—that any incursions made into their country have been produced by reiterated injuries committed by them—that the predatory mode of warfare they have carried on renders it difficult, and indeed impossible, to discriminate, or to ascertain to what tribe the offenders belong. Since my first visit to the district in November, 1783, I can venture to say that more than fifteen hundred persons have been killed and taken prisoners by the Indians; and upwards of twenty thousand horses have been taken away, with other property consisting of money, merchandize, household goods, wearing apparel, etc., of great value. The government has been repeatedly informed of those injuries, and that they continued to be perpetrated daily, notwithstanding which the people have received no satisfactory information whether the government intended to afford them relief or not. . . . I will, sir, be candid on this subject, not only as an inhabitant of Kentucky but as a friend to society who wishes to see order and regularity preserved in the government under which he lives. The people say they have groaned under their misfortunes—they see no prospect of relief—they constitute the strength and wealth of the western country, and yet all measures heretofore attempted have been committed for execution to the hands of strangers who have no interest in common with the west. They are the great sufferers and yet they have no voice in the matters which so vitally affect them. They are even accused of being the aggressors, and have no representative to state or to justify their conduct. These are the general sentiments of the western people who are beginning to want faith in the government, and appear determined to avenge themselves. For this purpose a meeting was lately held in this place by a number of respectable characters, to determine on the propriety of carrying on their expeditions this fall."

Kentucky was organized as a Territory this year (1790).

Early in June, 1790, when yet at Kaskaskia, Governor St. Clair received from Major Hamtramck a report of the failure of his and Gamelin's mission to the hostile Savages, and of the hopelessness of being able to make treaties for peace. Committing the resolutions of Congress relative to lands and settlers along the Wabash River to Winthrop Sargent, Secretary, who then proceeded to organize the county of Knox, St. Clair returned by way of the rivers to Fort Washington, where he arrived July 11th. Here General Harmar reported to him many raids and murders by the Savages, and

"it was agreed and determined that General Harmar should conduct an expedition against the Maumee River towns, the residence of all the renegade Indians, from whence issued all the parties who infest our frontiers. The Governor remained with us but three days. One thousand militia were ordered from Kentucky and the Governor on his way to New York the seat of the General Government, was to order five hundred from the back counties of Pennsylvania. The 15th September was the time appointed for the militia to assemble at Fort Washington."

Active preparations were instituted by General Harmar for this campaign, the object of which was, not only the present chastisement of the Savages, but the building of one or more forts along the Maumee River, and the establishing of a connecting line of refuge posts for supplies from which posts sorties could be made to intercept hostiles.

Governor St. Clair sent on September 19th from Marietta, "by a private gentleman," a letter to Major Patrick Murray, the British commandant at Detroit, reading in part as follows:

"This is to give you the fullest assurance of the pacific disposition entertained towards Great Britain and all her possessions [sic]; and to inform you explicitly that the expedition about to be undertaken is not intended against the post you have the honor to command. . . . After this candid explanation, sir, there is every reason to expect, both from your own personal character, and from the regard you have for that of our nation [sic], that those tribes will meet with neither countenance nor assistance from any under your command, and that you will do what in your power lies to restrain the trading people from whose instigations there is too good reasons to believe much of the injuries committed by the savages has proceeded."

The army gathered for the expedition marched northward from Fort Washington October 4, 1790, under command of General Josiah Harmar, Commander-in-Chief of the armies of the United States. It was composed of fourteen hundred and fifty-three soldiers, viz.: three hundred and twenty regulars, including one artillery company with three light brass cannon, the largest a six pounder, in two battalions; eleven hundred and thirty-three militia from Kentucky in four battalions, three of infantry and one of mounted riflemen; and one battalion from Pennsylvania. Most of these men were wholly unused to organized warfare, were poorly equipped, and were commanded by officers inclined to be rather discordant.

Colonel Hardin arrived with his command at the Miami village, at the head of the Maumee River, the site of the present city of Fort Wayne, Indiana, on October 16th, and took possession without opposition, the Savages having fled into the woods, upon being notified by their scouts of the approach of the army. The women and children went to their former retreats, and the warriors watched from their well chosen places for ambush attack. Upon the arrival of his part of the expedition, General Harmar determined to discover the place of the enemy's retreat, and to bring them to battle. The army was divided into detachments. The one following the main trail of the enemy became divided inadvertently, and met with a severe attack from ambush which entailed great loss. The reports of the militiamen returning promiscuously called forth a caustic order from General Harmar, reading in part as follows:

"The cause of the detachment being worsted yesterday was entirely owing to the shameful cowardly conduct of the militia who ran away and threw down their arms without firing scarcely a gun. In returning to Fort Washington if any officer or man shall presume to quit the ranks, or not to march in the form that they are ordered, the General will assuredly order the artillery to fire on them."

The remaining part of the army started on its return to Fort Washington, after destroying all the buildings and food supplies that could well be found. At the first encampment, seven miles from the destroyed Miami villages, Colonel Hardin, desiring to retrieve his lost prestige by dealing the Savages a heavy blow, to prevent, at least, their following and harassing the returning army, prevailed upon General Harmar to give him a detachment of four hundred men with which to go back in the night to the site of the towns and attack the Savages that, doubtless, had returned there. This request was granted.

Three hundred and forty militiamen under Colonel Hardin, and sixty regular troops under Major Wyllys, started in time to arrive at the river about break of day, October 22d. They were late in arriving. The enemy had returned as expected. The plan of attack was carefully outlined; but some failure to obey orders, and unexpected ambuscades by the Savages, which divided the command, resulted again in a most disastrous defeat for the Americans. As in the first defeat, the regulars lost most of their men, including Major Wyllys. The loss among the Savages was thought to be about as large as that of the Americans.

General Harmar could not be prevailed upon by Colonel Hardin to return to the river with all his remaining army. His reply was:

"We are now scarcely able to move our baggage; it would take up three days to go, and return to this place; we have no more forage for our horses; the Indians have got a very good scourging; and I will keep the army in perfect readiness to receive them if they think best to follow."

The American loss in this expedition was one hundred and eighty-three killed, and thirty-one wounded. General Harmar, annoyed by adverse criticism of his conduct of the expedition, asked President Washington, March 28, 1791, for a board of officers to act as a Court of Inquiry. This request was granted and, after considering the evidence, he was acquitted of any fault.

Nothing was said about his failure to build the

forts that had been thought desirable. Some of the officials, however, had urged objections to the suggested forts in the wilderness, such as the cost of their maintenance with garrisons and supplies, and their rather limited efficiency. But General Harmar's command was prepared for such work, and was not prepared for aggressive warfare, as the sequel proved. Had he built a strong fort at the head of the Maumee River immediately upon his arrival there, and had he garnered, instead of burning, the products of the fields, and, upon his return, left a chain of such forts, these would have been rallying points where the soldiers might have kept the Savages away from the British influences while teaching them to favor those who were the rightful owners of their hunting grounds, rightfully so by repeated conquest and by treaty purchases from different tribes. These forts would also have been rallying points for the commissioners of peace to these Savages, as well as for those Savages who would gradually, one by one, and tribe by tribe, have been won over to lead peaceful lives. The moral and physical effects of such forts were later demonstrated, when the authorities in the East came to the realization that they were a necessity.

General Harmar resigned his commission the

following January, and was made Adjutant-General of Pennsylvania in 1793, in which position he rendered good service in furnishing troops for General Wayne's army in 1794.

The Savages were greatly elated at their successes in defeating General Harmar's army. Like the ancient Romans who returned home to celebrate their great victories in triumphal processions, these Savages went to Detroit, the headquarters of their masters and allies, the British, where they daily paraded the streets uttering their demoniac scalp yells, while bearing long poles strung with the scalps of the many American soldiers they had killed. Additional war parties of Savages were soon started for the American frontier settlements.

The British, also, were elated at the successes of the Savages, exhibiting their pleasure by words condemnatory of the American policy, and by inciting the Savages to further atrocities.

The anxiety, always present with the frontier settlers, now increased to a panic. The officers, local and general, whose duty it was to guard and protect legitimate settlers, had often been remiss in their duties; they were, probably, often without the necessary power. While their physical resources were deficient, they had been wanting, too, perhaps, in a broad comprehension of the requirements, and had been dilatory in obtaining the means that would have begotten from the first more unity of effort and strength of resistance to the treacherous Savages, while they were formulating broader and more definite plans for overcoming their savagery by stopping the British aid and abetment of it. Now the American authorities became even more disconcerted than before, and their efforts to protect the settlements with soldiers grew even more spasmodic. The sending of agents to placate the Savages at this inopportune time, when another army sufficient in size to overcome them was being recruited for the building of forts throughout the forests,—those forests which the Savages had been taught by the French and British never to give up to the Americans, and in their determination to retain which they were yet being sustained by the British,—was again being pointed out by the British and Savages as an evidence of American insincerity and duplicity. Such was the result of the long-continued pacific policy of the American officials, if any policy could be said to have existed, toward the intriguing British first, and the Savages afterwards! Their efforts had only occasionally been awakened, with mere temporizing effect on the enemies, to react severely upon the settlements!

CHAPTER VI

OVERWHELMING SUCCESS OF THE ENEMY

More Troops Gathered for Defence—Messenger Sent to the Senecas for Peace Agents—British Opposition—Expedition against Hostile Savages Successful—Army Gathered for Decisive Blow to the Marauding Savages—Commanded by General, and Governor, St. Clair, it Meets Overwhelming Defeat—Women with the Army.

THE Legislature of Virginia, December 20, 1790, authorized Governor Beverly Randolph to provide for the enlistment of several companies of rangers before the 1st of March for the protection of the frontier; and Charles Scott was appointed Brigadier-General of Kentucky militia.

Early in January, 1791, that more attention and deference should be given to the West, Congress appointed General Scott, Henry Inness, John Brown, Benjamin Logan, and Isaac Shelby a Board of War for the District of Kentucky, with discretionary powers.

The 3d of March Congress also made provision for another regiment of Federal troops, and for raising two thousand militia for six months' service, as a further protection of the frontier; and President Washington immediately appointed Governor, and General, Arthur St. Clair Commander-in-Chief of this Army of the Northwest.

Colonel Thomas Proctor was sent March 12, 1791, to the Seneca tribe of the Six Nations of New York to enlist from them peace agents to the western tribes; but the British at Niagara would not permit a boat to take these agents across Lake Erie in the interest of the United States. Also, by the endeavors of the British, and Colonel Brant, false reports were circulated, that the United States was endeavoring to involve the Six Nations in war with the western tribes.

Further evidence of this continued British policy to dominate all of the American Aborigines was given in the communications of the British officers to them, and in the Aborigines deferring to their request that all questions of moment should be referred to the British.

Radical military operations against the Savages' retreats appearing necessary, and the result of Colonel Proctor's mission for the intercession of the Six Nations for peace having been awaited as long as practicable, General Scott, with eight hundred cavalry, crossed the Ohio River on May 23, 1791, at the mouth of the Kentucky River, and started for the historic Ouiotenon, situated by the Wabash River near the present city of Lafayette, Indiana. Rain fell in torrents with much high wind, but the troops arrived at their destination the 1st of June after an estimated march of one hundred and sixty miles through the forest with only varying trails for road. The last of the Savages were just leaving the proximal town when General, now acting Lieutenant-Colonel, James Wilkinson pressed forward with the First Battalion and "destroyed all the Savages with which five canoes were crowded."

There was a Kickapoo town on the north bank of the river from which a brisk firing was directed at the troops. The river was at flood and soldiers were sent above and below to effect a crossing, which was done by swimming, and the Savages were dislodged. Meantime Colonel Hardin's command had discovered a stronger village on the left which they surprised, killing six Savages and taking fifty-two prisoners. The next evening Colonel Wilkinson started with three hundred and sixty men on foot, and early the next morning they assailed and destroyed the important town of Kethtipecanunk at the mouth of Eel River eighteen miles above Ouiotenon, returning from this thirty-six miles' walk and work in twelve hours. All the villages and supplies that could be found were destroyed. General Scott reported that:

"Many of the inhabitants of this village [Ouiotenon] were French and lived in a state of civilization. By the books, letters, and other documents found here it is evident that the place was in close connection with and dependent on Detroit. A large quantity of corn, a variety of household goods, peltry, and other articles were burned with this village which consisted of about seventy houses, many of them well finished."[1]

On June 4th, General Scott set free sixteen of his prisoners who were in poor condition to withstand the march, giving to their care a well-worded letter, addressed to all the tribes along the Wabash, requesting peace, and informing where his retained prisoners could be found.

The severe rains and the swollen condition of the streams, with his forced marches through the almost trackless forest, had disabled his horses and, his supplies being depleted, he reluctantly directed the march southward instead of toward the Maumee River, and arrived at the Rapids of the Ohio

[1] *See American State Papers, Indian Affairs*, volume i, page 129.

June 14th. He reported no death in his command and only five wounded, while of Savages thirty-two were killed and fifty-eight taken prisoners, of which the forty-two not liberated were given to the care of Captain Asheton of the First United States Regiment at Fort Steuben. No Frenchmen were captured, if seen, and no scalps were taken.

General St. Clair recommended another expedition to the Eel River to weaken those tribes which would ally themselves with the Miamis against his army then forming for the purpose of laying waste the strongholds, and establishing a series of forts in the Maumee country. Accordingly Colonel Wilkinson, with five hundred and twenty-five cavalry, started from the vicinity of Fort Washington to the northward, "feinting boldly at the Miami Villages," and then turned northwestward to the Wabash near the mouth of Eel River. The evening of the sixth day he captured the Savages' most important town in this vicinity, known by the French name L'Anguille — the Eel. This expedition then ranged along the Wabash River, passed through the site of Ouiotenon, thence along General Scott's route, and arrived at the Rapids of the Ohio August 21st, having travelled four hundred and fifty miles, destroyed several villages and more than four hundred acres of corn; captured thirty-four or more Savage prisoners and killed ten or more others. One American prisoner was recovered. Two soldiers were killed and one wounded. Colonel Wilkinson also left behind some infirm Aborigines, unharmed, to whom he gave a letter, addressed to the different tribes, urging them to accept the favorable terms of peace still offered to them. This, as well as the former letter, was taken to the British, who gave their own desired rendering of it to the Aborigines; and the warriors were incited to greater efforts in their savage work.

General Harmar predicted defeat for General St. Clair's army which, with great difficulties, was being gathered to operate along the Maumee River. This army was not ready to advance until September 17, 1791. Then, about twenty-three hundred soldiers, including regulars, moved from the vicinity of Fort Washington and built Fort Hamilton on the west bank of the Miami River at the site of the present city of Hamilton, Ohio. Again advancing under command of General St. Clair, they began to build Fort Jefferson, six miles south of the present city of Greenville, October 12th. Twelve days later the march again began, but the progress was very slow.

The evening of the 3d of November the army encamped by the Wabash River about one mile and a half east of the present Ohio-Indiana State line. During the night there were many Savages near the pickets, and much firing of the pickets' guns. About ten o'clock that night General Butler, who commanded the right wing, was requested to send out an intelligent officer with a detachment of soldiers to reconnoitre. He detailed Captain Slough, two subalterns, and thirty men of the line for this purpose, but nothing alarming was discovered.

Early the next morning, the army, then numbering about fourteen hundred regular and militia soldiers, and eighty-six officers, was furiously assailed by about the same number of Savages, and it went down to the most disastrous defeat ever suffered by such large numbers from such foe. General St. Clair's Adjutant, Ebenezer Denny, thus describes the scenes:

"The troops paraded this morning, 4 November, 1791, at the usual time, and had been dismissed from the lines but a few minutes, the sun not yet up, when the woods in front rung with the yells and [gun] fire of the savages. The poor militia, who were but three hundred yards in front, had scarcely time to return a shot—they fled into our camp. The troops were under arms in an instant, and a smart fire from the front line met the enemy. It was but a few minutes, however, until the men were engaged in every quarter. The enemy from the front filed off to the right and left, and completely surrounded the camp, killed and cut off nearly all the guards, and approached close to the lines. They advanced from one tree, log, or stump to another, under cover of the smoke of our fire. Our artillery and musketry made a tremendous noise huddled together as they were but did little execution. The Aborigines seemed to brave everything, and when fairly fixed around us they made no noise other than their fire [guns] which they kept up very constant and which seldom failed to tell, although scarcely heard.

"Our left flank, probably from the nature of the ground, gave way first; the enemy got possession of that part of the encampment but, it being pretty clear ground, they were too much exposed and were soon repulsed. I was at this time with the General [St. Clair] engaged toward the right; he was on foot and led the party himself that drove the enemy and regained our ground on the left. The battalions in the rear charged several times and forced the Savages from their shelter, but they always turned with the battalions and fired upon their backs; indeed they seemed not to fear anything we could do. They could skip out of reach of the bayonet and return, as they pleased. They were visible only when raised by a charge.

"The ground was literally covered with the dead. The wounded were taken to the centre, where it was thought most safe, and where a great many who had quit their posts unhurt had crowded together. The General, with other officers, endeavored to rally these

men, and twice they were taken out to the lines.
It appeared that the officers had been singled out; a
very great proportion fell, or were wounded and were
obliged to retire from the lines early in the action.
General Butler was among the latter, as well as several other of the most experienced officers. The men,
being thus left with few officers, became fearful,
despaired of success, gave up the fight, and to save
themselves for the moment, abandoned entirely their
duty and ground, and crowded in toward the centre of
the field, and no exertions could put them in any order
even for defence; they became perfectly ungovernable.
The enemy at length got possession of the artillery,
though not until the officers were all killed but one
and he badly wounded, and the men [gunners] almost
all cut off, and not until the pieces were spiked.

"As our lines were deserted the Aborigines contracted
theirs until their shot centred from all points, and
now meeting with little opposition, took more deliberate aim and did great execution. Exposed to a cross
fire, men and officers were seen falling in every direction; the distress, too, of the wounded made the scene
such as can scarcely be conceived—a few minutes
longer, and a retreat would have been impossible—
the only hope left was, that perhaps the Savages
would be so taken up with the camp as not to follow.
Delay was death; no preparation could be made;
numbers of brave men must be left a sacrifice, there
was no alternative. It was past nine o'clock when
repeated orders were given to charge toward the road.
The action had continued between two and three
hours. Both officers and men seemed confounded,
incapable of doing anything; they could not move
until it was told that a retreat was intended. A few

officers put themselves in front, the men followed, the enemy gave way, and perhaps not being aware of the design, we were for a few minutes left undisturbed. The stoutest and most active now took the lead, and those who were foremost in breaking the enemy's line were soon left behind.

"At the moment of the retreat one of the few horses saved had been procured for the General; he was on foot until then; I kept by him, and he delayed to see the rear. The enemy soon discovered the movement and pursued, though not more than four or five miles, and but few so far; they turned to share the spoil. Soon after the firing ceased I was directed to endeavor to gain the front and, if possible, to cause a short halt that the rear might get up. I had been on horseback from the first alarm, and well mounted; and now pushed forward, but met with so many difficulties and interruptions from the people that I was two hours at least laboring to reach the front. With the assistance of two or three officers I caused a short halt; but the men grew impatient and would move on. I got Lieutenants Sedam and Morgan, with half a dozen stout men, to fill up the road and to move slowly; I halted myself until the General came up. By this time the remains of the army had got somewhat compact, but in the most miserable and defenceless state. The wounded who came off left their arms in the field, and one half of the others threw theirs away on the retreat. The road for miles was covered with firelocks [flintlock guns], cartridge boxes, and regimentals. How fortunate that the pursuit was discontinued; a single Savage might have followed with safety upon either flank. Such a panic had seized the men that I believe it would not have been possible to have brought any of them to engage again.

"In the afternoon Lieutenant Kersey with a detachment of the First Regiment met us. This regiment, the only complete and best disciplined portion of the army, had been ordered back upon the road on the 31st October. They were thirty miles from the battle ground when they heard distinctly the firing of the cannon, were hastening forward, and had marched about nine miles when met by some of the militia who informed Major Hamtramck, the commanding officer, that the army was totally destroyed. The Major judged it best to send on a subaltern to obtain some knowledge of things, and to return himself with the regiment to Fort Jefferson eight miles back, and to secure at all events that post. He had made some arrangements, and as we arrived in the evening, found him preparing again to meet us. Stragglers continued to come in for hours after we reached the fort.

"The remnant of the army, with the First Regiment, were now at Fort Jefferson, twenty-nine miles from the field of action, without provisions, and the former without having eaten anything for twenty-four hours. A convoy was known to be upon the road, and within a day's march. The General determined to move with the First Regiment, and all the levies [militia] able to march. Those of the wounded and others unable to go on were lodged as comfortably as possible within the fort. Accordingly we set out a little after ten and continued our route until within an hour of daylight, then halted and waited for day and until the rear came up. Moved on again about nine o'clock; the morning of the 5th we met the convoy; stopped a sufficiency to subsist us to Fort Hamilton; sent the remainder on to Jefferson under an additional escort of a captain and sixty men; proceeded, and at first water halted, partly cooked and eat for the first time since the night preceding the action. At one o'clock moved on, and continued our route until nine at night when we halted and made fires within fifteen miles of Fort Hamilton. Marched again just before day, the General soon after rode on to the fort. Troops reached there in the afternoon.

"November 7, 1791. Fort Hamilton command was ordered off with a small supply for the wounded, etc. About twelve same day continued our march, and halted before night within fifteen miles of Fort Washington, which place we reached the afternoon of the eighth.

" The prediction of defeat by General Harmar before the army set out on the campaign was founded upon his experience and particular knowledge of things. He saw with what material the army was composed; men collected from the streets and prisons of the cities, hurried out into the enemy's country, and with the officers commanding them totally unacquainted with the business in which they were engaged, it was utterly impossible they could be otherwise than defeated. Besides, not any one department was sufficiently prepared; both quartermaster and the contractors extremely deficient. It was a matter of astonishment to him [General Harmar] that the commanding general [St. Clair], who was acknowledged to be perfectly competent, should think of hazarding with such people and under such circumstances, his reputation and life, and the lives of so many others, knowing too, as both did, the enemy with whom he was going to contend; an enemy brought up from infancy to war, and perhaps superior to an equal number of the best men that could be taken against them. It is a truth, I had hopes that the noise and show which the army made on their march might deter the enemy from attempting a serious and general attack. It was unfortunate that both the general officers were, and had been, disabled by sickness; in such situation it is possible that some essential matters might be overlooked. The Adjutant-General, Colonel Winthrop Sargent, an old Revolutionary officer, was, however, constantly on the alert; he took upon himself the burden of everything, and a very serious and troublesome task he had. But one most important object was wanting, can't say neglected, but more might have been done toward obtaining it; this was a knowledge of the collected force and situation of the enemy; of this we were perfectly ignorant. Some few scouts out, but no great distance. . . ."

In this overwhelming defeat General St. Clair's army lost five hundred and ninety-three privates killed and missing. Thirty-nine officers were killed, including Major-General Richard Butler, one lieutenant-colonel, three majors, twelve captains, ten lieutenants, eight ensigns, two quartermasters, one adjutant, and Surgeon Grasson. Thirty-one officers and two hundred and fifty-two privates were wounded. The artillery and all supplies, including clothing, two hundred tents, three hundred horses, one hundred and thirty beef cattle, and food in the wagons, with muskets and other equipment thrown away by many stricken soldiers, all valued at $32,810.75, were left to be gathered by the highly elated Savages, who took to their lodges by the Maumee, Auglaize, and other rivers all they could transport.

On account of necessary delays, the cold weather, and bad roads, it required six weeks for St. Clair's aide, Lieutenant Denny, to convey on horseback the news of this crushing defeat to the office of the Secretary of War, General Knox, in Philadelphia.

President Washington was greatly distressed by the news. General St. Clair requested the appointment of a Court of Inquiry regarding the defeat. This was done by the War Department, and the Court exonerated him. He resigned his commission March 5, 1792. He was, however, further retained as Governor of the Territory, which many prominent men in the Territory thought another great mistake.

The principal causes of the failure of the expedition, as recorded in the Secretary of War's office, are: "1st. The deficient number of good troops, according to the expectation in the early part of the year. 2d. Their want of sufficient discipline, according to the nature of the service. 3rd. The lateness of the season."

The wet and cold weather, with thin ice and snow, certainly added much to the inefficiency of the volunteers who were unused to such campaigning, and added greatly to their sufferings in defeat. Certainly the illness of General St. Clair should not be urged as an excuse for the laxity in fortifying and reconnoitering by his subordinates.

There were other unwise features of this expedition associated with undisciplined soldiers and incompetent officers. The wives and women of many soldiers were with the army. They were favored as much as practicable, but many of them were killed by the Savages.[1]

General Wilkinson visited this field of slaughter about the last of January, 1792, with one hundred and fifty-two volunteer cavalrymen, some of whom were frost-bitten on the way from Fort Jefferson. From the distance of about four miles from the site of the encampment they found scattered along the way the remains of Americans who had been pursued and killed, or who had died of their wounds while endeavoring to escape. The field of action was thickly strewn with remnants

---

[1] Caleb Atwater writes in his *History of the State of Ohio*, 1838, that there were with this army at the commencement of the attack of the Savages about two hundred and fifty women, of whom fifty-six were killed. But few escaped death or captivity.

From 1790-1792

of human bodies showing horrible mutilations by the Savages. Sand and clay were found packed into the eyes and throats, done probably while the wounded were alive; limbs were found separated from bodies; and stakes the size of arms were found driven through the bodies of women. The flesh had been stripped from many bones, but the relative part done by the savage cannibals and the wolves could not be determined. The latter were yet at work.

As many of these remains as possible on account of the snow and cold weather were gathered and buried in shallow trenches dug with difficulty in the frozen ground by the benumbed soldiers. Three whole cannon carriages were found and removed to Fort Jefferson; the other five were in damaged condition. All the cannon were missing.[1]

---

[1] General Wayne's army gathered and buried all bones that could be found on and around this field Christmas week, 1793, previous to the building of Fort Recovery. Six hundred skulls were counted.—*American Pioneer*, 1842, volume i, page 294.

CHAPTER VII

FURTHER NEFARIOUS WORK CULMINATING

Great Efforts of British Allies—Distress of Frontier Settlements—British Fear Loss of Fur Trade—Advance of Civil Jurisdiction—General Wayne Chosen to Lead Another Army against the Hostiles—Further Treaties with the Aborigines—Secret Efforts to Learn Status of the British—Largest Council of Savages for British Confederation—Kentucky Admitted as a State—Forts Built by Americans—Commissioners Appointed to Attend the Great Council—Their Object Defeated by the British—Specific Charges of Fraud and Force by British Presented to the British Minister.

THE British and their savage allies did not want the peace that the Americans would have accepted previous to the defeat of General Harmar's army; much less would they comply with the proclamation of Governor St. Clair, or respond favorably to various other peace overtures made to them after this disaster. They rallied all the available warriors of the different tribes nearby—the Miamis under Chief Little Turtle, the Delawares under

Buckongehelas, the Shawnees under Blue Jacket, the Ottawas, Wyandots, Pottawotamis, Kickapoos, and bands of lesser significance—against the coming of General St. Clair; and the easy destruction of this, the second large army, commanded by the Governor—to them, the great American chieftain,—was to them the cause of extreme joy. This, their second great success, with the largely increased number of scalps and other rich spoils gathered from their victims, was looked upon as full license for a continuance of their raids on the settlements, and as an omen of their ultimate success, on the plan of Pontiac in 1763, in driving the Americans from the western country.

The American frontier settlements, with, if possible, increased apprehension, sent more urgent petitions to the authorities for protection. Some of these petitions represented that not less than fifteen hundred Kentuckians—men, women, and children—had been slain or carried into captivity by the Savages within seven years; that the frontier settlements of Pennsylvania and Virginia had suffered nearly as much; and that the prospect was now more gloomy than before, as the enemy was, if possible, more aggressive and savage.

On the other hand, the allies of the Savages, the British, were becoming more apprehensive regarding their fur trade on account of the depletion of their allies, the Savages, by American armies. The defeat of two armies was sure to be followed by another army, stronger and more destructive. The Montreal merchants whose lucrative trade with the American Savages had lessened during the more active hostilities, on December 9, 1791, petitioned Colonel John Graves Simcoe, Lieutenant-Governor of Upper Canada, for protection; and suggested closer union with the Savages, and a continued retention of the American forts yet occupied by the British.

Secretary of War Henry Knox, "in obedience to the command" of President Washington, made, on the 26th of December, an interesting statement relative to the frontiers northwest of the Ohio River, which includes the following paragraph, viz:

"Hence it would appear that the principles of justice as well as policy and, it may be added, the principles of economy, all combine to dictate that an adequate military force should be raised as soon as possible, placed upon the frontiers, and disciplined according to the nature of the service, in order to meet with the prospect of success against the greatest probable combination of the enemy."

Messages and overtures for peace were again

sent to the various tribes of Aborigines, including the Six Nations; and preparations for the proposed army were also entered upon.

To advance the civil jurisdiction as much as possible, Hamilton County was, February 11, 1792, extended by Governor St. Clair, who yet retained his civil office, eastward to the Scioto River, and northward to the territorial limits in Lake Erie.

President Washington having been greatly disappointed in the result of the expedition of General St. Clair, who was a former member of his military staff, made the selection of the commander for the proposed campaign with great circumspection. Generals Anthony Wayne, Henry Lee, Daniel Morgan, Andrew Pickens, Rufus Putnam, Charles Scott, James Wilkinson, and Alexander McGillivray were those of most prominence from whom to choose; and Anthony Wayne was selected early in 1792. The result showed the wisdom of the choice, notwithstanding the statement of General Lee that this appointment "caused extreme disgust among all orders in the Old Dominion."

Soon after this appointment, General Wayne issued a proclamation to acquaint the anxious frontiersmen with the efforts in progress to secure peace by treaty, and to request all persons to avoid all action that would further anger the Aborigines. The governors of Virginia and Pennsylvania issued similar proclamations.

Major John F. Hamtramck effected, at Vincennes in March, 1792, treaties with small bands of the Wabash and Eel River tribes, and he also sent peace messages to those of the Maumee River. About fifty chiefs of the Six Nations visited Philadelphia by invitation, and accepted the overtures for peace.

On April 7th, General Wilkinson sent two messengers, Freeman and Girard, with peace messages to the Miamis of the Maumee River; and, on the 20th of May, Colonel John Hardin and Major Alexander Truman started northward on like missions—but not one of the four returned to tell of the savage treatment, and death, they suffered.

General Putnam on the 27th of September succeeded in closing terms of peace with thirty-one Aborigines of the Wabash and Illinois tribes at Vincennes. Each of the parties to these peace negotiations carried copies of the treaties of 1784, '85, '86, '89, and many expressions and assurances by the Americans to turn the Savages from their work of carnage. But all availed nothing with the strong tribes who claimed to be directly under influence and command of the British, and the murderous raids by the Savages continued unabated.

Of the secret efforts to learn more of detail regarding the relations between the Savages and the British, to be the better able therefrom to appease the former, but one succeeded, on account of the great vigilance of both parties to the alliance. William May was started from Fort Hamilton May 13, 1792, to follow on the trail of Major Truman. He was captured by Savages, as expected, and after escaping many dangers was taken along the Maumee River, and sold to Matthew Elliott, then British Assistant Agent to the Aborigines, from whose service he finally escaped and gave sworn testimony before General Wayne at Pittsburg, October 11, 1792. This evidence detailed different items of interest, among which are the following:

There were gathered in the summer of 1792 by the Maumee River at the mouth of the Auglaize, then the headquarters of several tribes, three thousand and six hundred warriors of many tribes, and more were arriving at the time of May's sojourn there, all of whom received daily rations from the British authorities at Detroit.

This was the largest council of Aborigines on record, and it appeared to the British as the culmination of their hopes, and long-continued endeavors, for the confederation of all the American tribes regardless of American interests.

The Seneca Chief Cornplanter and forty-eight other chiefs of the Six Nations of New York were, in the interests of peace, representing the Americans at this council; and Chief Cornplanter reported to General Wayne that: ... "we cannot tell the names of the nations present. There were present three men from the Gora[1] nations; it took them a whole season to come; and twenty-seven nations [tribes] from beyond Canada. The whole of them know that we, the Six Nations, have General Washington by the hand." This reference to General Washington was relative to their recent visit to Philadelphia, and the peace treaty there effected. Other tribes were expected at this grand council at the mouth of the Auglaize River, and they came later, from the extreme South and West. A like council was called for the next year, and, later, runners were sent with invitations to the most distant tribes in all directions, including the

---

[1] Gora, or Gorah, was one of the names formerly given by the Six Nations (Iroquois) of New York to Sir William Johnson and to Colonel Guy Johnson; and these Gora Aborigines were probably of the Iroquois of Canada who were at this time under the control of Sir John Johnson, British Superintendent of Indian Affairs.

Creeks and Cherokees of the South, urging their attendance.

William May, as he had been a sailor, was kept by his purchaser three months in the transportation service, on board a schooner carrying a load of about one hundred and sixty barrels between Detroit and the foot of the Maumee Rapids, many miles within United States territory, where was situated the great supply house of the British Aborigine Agent Alexander McKee, from whom the Savages received their food, supplies of firearms, ammunition, scalping knives, tomahawks, etc., with which to raid and murder Americans wherever possible.

Kentucky was admitted into the Union as a State June 1, 1792, thus giving her the representation she richly deserved.

A number of small forts were built by the Americans along the frontier as bases for supplies and places of refuge for the remaining settlers.

In addition to the attacks on individuals and families along the borders, a company of mounted Kentucky riflemen under Major John Adair, on November 6, 1792, near Post St. Clair, about twenty-five miles north of Fort Hamilton, Ohio, was suddenly attacked by a party of Savages who exhibited "a degree of courage that bespoke them warriors indeed" reads the report of the Major. Six Americans were killed, five wounded, and four missing. The Savages also killed a number of pack-horses and captured others. Their loss was thought to be about the same as that of the Kentuckians.

At this time, the army being formed by General Wayne was encamped twenty-two miles below Pittsburg, both to protect the Virginia frontier, and to give opportunity for drilling and disciplining the men.

For the purpose of continuing the efforts to secure peace with the Savages by further treaty, President Washington, March 2, 1793, appointed General Benjamin Lincoln of Massachusetts, Beverly Randolph of Virginia, and Timothy Pickering of Pennsylvania, Commissioners, to attend the great council to be held in American territory at the foot of the lowest Rapids of the Maumee, or at Sandusky, the 1st of June.

On May 17th, Messrs. Randolph and Pickering arrived at Fort Niagara, and there received a note from Lieutenant-Governor and Colonel John Graves Simcoe inviting them to become guests at his home, Navy Hall, nearly a mile from the fort; and there being no other suitable place for them to stop, the invitation was accepted. General Lincoln arrived May 25th.

Meantime a letter was received from Colonel McKee, British Indian Agent at Detroit, stating that the tribal councils by the Maumee would probably not end before the latter part of June and that the Commissioners had best remain at Niagara until he notified them that the Aborigines were ready to receive them.

Colonel John Butler, a leader in the Wyoming Massacre in July, 1778, now a British Superintendent of Aborigine Affairs, and Captain Joseph Brant of like notoriety, with a picked company of fifty Savages, arrived at Niagara, July 5th. They came from the large collection of tribes then at the British distributing house at the foot of the Maumee Rapids, and requested an explanation of the "unfair and unwarrantable" warlike preparations of General Wayne; and they desired to know the authority for the trespassing of the Americans north of the Ohio River, all of which they claimed as territory belonging to the Aborigines. The Commissioners in reply cited in explanation the several treaties of previous years, and the subsequent maraudings of the Savages, and expressed desire for peace; and an agreement was made to meet in full council at Sandusky.

The Commissioners were permitted to leave Niagara July 10th and, awaiting a favorable wind, the British sloop on which they were passengers sailed from Fort Erie, opposite the present city of Buffalo, on the 14th, and arrived at the mouth of the Detroit River or Strait the 21st. They were received, and entertained during their enforced stay there of nearly four weeks, by Captain Matthew Elliott, British Assistant Agent for and to the Aborigines. So had they been with Simcoe, and yet were, in fact, prisoners of the British. They continued frequently to urge an early meeting of the council according to agreement, without satisfactory reply.

On July 29th, a deputation of over twenty Aborigines, with the notorious Simon Girty as interpreter, arrived at Captain Elliott's house from the grand council that had been for weeks assembled at the foot of the Maumee Rapids. After a brief preliminary, they presented to the Commissioners a short written communication, ostensibly from the council, the principal sentence of which was that, "If you seriously design to make a firm and lasting peace, you will immediately remove all your people from our side of that river" (the Ohio). The Commissioners delivered to them in writing a long and carefully prepared reply in which the treaties

From 1792-1793 89

of 1768, '84, '85, '86, and '89 were referred to in justification of the advance of Americans into the territory north of the Ohio River, and with reasons why it was impossible at this late date to make this river the boundary; stating that the United States government was willing to make liberal concessions to the Aborigines, as the treaty with Great Britain declared the middle of the Great Lakes and the waters which unite them to be the boundary of the United States; and they closed the reply expressing the desire to meet the general council in treaty soon.

On the 8th and 9th of August, the Commissioners received verbal and chance reports that all the tribes represented at the Maumee council were for peace, with the exception of the Shawnees, Wyandots, Miamis, and Delawares, and that these were yielding; that many were tired of the long delays and were departing for their respective villages. The Commissioners again expressed strong desire to go directly to the Maumee council, which meeting was well within American territory; but such action the British would not permit. On August 14th the American Commissioners wrote to the chiefs at the council, again urging a meeting for a treaty. They also wrote to Colonel McKee at that place, stating that his aid for such result would be gratefully acknowledged. On the 16th, a long and carefully written reply was received at Captain Elliott's house by the Commissioners, which closed with the assertion that, if they would not agree to the Ohio River being the boundary, "a meeting would be altogether unnecessary." Appended to this paper were written the following names of "Nations" represented, viz.: Wyandots, Seven Nations of Canada, Delawares, Shawnees, Miamis, Ottawas, Chippewas, Senecas of the Glaise [Auglaize River], Pottawotamis, Connoys, Munsees, Nantakokias, Mohicans, Messasagoes, Creeks, Cherokees.

This communication, like the others, was understood to be fully conceived and written by the British authorities; and it was certainly approved by their censors. This general council, as well as the one the year before by the Maumee River at the mouth of the Auglaize, was the result of British efforts for many years to federate all the Savages, as Simcoe stated that their dictated decision in council, and united action in war, might become irresistible to the Americans. Joseph Brant, leader in the Six Nations and generally a stanch friend of the British, declared that such united action: "caused the defeat of two American armies [Harmar's and St. Clair's]. . . But to our sur-

From 1792-1793

prise, when upon the point of entering upon a treaty with the [American] Commissioners, we found that it was opposed by those acting under the British Government."

In reply to the ex-parte council's last communication, the Commissioners regretfully sent to the chiefs and to the British Colonel McKee the statement that their efforts for negotiations were at an end; including with the letters copies of the former treaties.

On August 23d the Commissioners, on their return, arrived by British boat opposite Fort Erie, where they dispatched, by different runners, a letter to General Wayne, and another to General Knox, Secretary of War, announcing their failure to secure terms of peace.

A portrayal of grievances and claims against Great Britain was formally presented this year (1793), by the United States authorities to the British Minister, Hammond, and request for redress. The main points of this document are abstracted as follows:

"The continued unjustifiable occupancy by the British of military posts within United States territory.

"The officers of these posts exercising jurisdiction over the country and inhabitants around these posts.

"The exclusion of citizens of the United States from

navigating the waters inside the United States line named in the Treaty of Paris.

"The intercepting of commerce with the Aborigines; which commerce should have been of great profit to the United States and her citizens not only on account of its intrinsic worth, but also because of its value as a means of insuring peace with the Aborigines, and of superseding the necessity for expensive warfare with them.

"Also, that upon the withdrawal of the British troops from New York after the Treaty of Paris, in violation of this Treaty a large embarkation of Negroes, property of the inhabitants of the United States, had taken place before the Commissioners for inspecting and superintending embarkations on the part of the United States had arrived there; and that the British had not rendered any account thereof.

"That nearly three thousand other Negroes were publicly carried away by the avowed order of the British commanding officer, and under the view and against the remonstrances of the Commissioners.

"That a very great number of Negroes were also carried away in private vessels, if not by the express permission of, yet certainly without opposition on the part of, the commanding officer who alone had the means of preventing it, and without admitting the inspection of the American Commissioners.

"That, of other species of property carried away, the commanding officer permitted no examination."

In support of these charges, specific documents of proof were attached. Other questions of serious nature also accompanied these charges of violation of the Treaty of Paris, and of great defraudings of citizens of the United States.

After the lapse of some months, Minister Hammond presented to Secretary Jefferson a series of charges that British creditors had been delayed in obtaining payment of their accounts; of alleged "unjust prosecutions, confiscations, and denials of justice in which British merchants and other of his Majesty's subjects [Tories] had suffered irreparable injury."

To these charges, Secretary Jefferson soon returned what the British called "a bulky and ingenious document" written in his direct and forceful style which quite filled them with dismay. It showed the British as by far the first, and greatest, transgressors, and that they should make redress. Hammond sent the document to the British Home Office, and there it rested. A year later Jefferson inquired regarding the matter, and received an indifferent answer. Another inquiry, after a lapse of several months, was met in a rather disdainful way. Hammond professed to get a little sympathy from Alexander Hamilton, then Secretary of the Treasury. It does not appear why a committee was not chosen to arbitrate the matter. It is evident that the British were satisfied with the advantages they possessed; and that most of the

Americans in authority were inclined to let the questions rest as they were, rather than to bring about another war with Great Britain.

The animus of the British at this time is described in the following excerpt from the late writings of one of their loyal subjects, viz.:

"The negotiations between England and the United States were destined to stand still until the former should be able to judge, from the progress of events, the safest course to pursue. Not only the unsettled state of the government in America, but the notorious jealousy and the hardly concealed animosity of several European nations, manifested in their attitude toward England, made it her business to look strictly and cautiously after her own interests."

CHAPTER VIII

RETRIBUTIVE JUSTICE MARCHES ON AGAINST GREAT OPPOSITION

Advance of General Wayne's Army—Opposed by the Enemy—Builds Forts Greenville and Recovery—Cause of British Aggressiveness yet More Apparent—Other Enemies of the United States—Separation of the Ohio Country from the United States again Suggested—British Build Two Additional Forts within United States Territory—Protests of the United States of no Avail—British and their Savage Allies Attack Fort Recovery and Are Repulsed—Further Account of Great Britain's Guiding Hand.

GENERAL WAYNE believed that further delay would be an undue exposure of the frontier to savage incursions and, October 5, 1793, he reported to the Secretary of War, from near Fort Washington, that his available army remained small from Kentucky disappointments, from fevers among his enlisted men, and from "the influenza [later called in America by the French name La Grippe] which has pervaded the whole line in a most alarming and rapid degree. . . . This is not a pleasant picture, but something must be done immediately to save the frontiers from impending savage fury. I will therefore advance to-morrow with the force I have in order to gain a strong position about six miles in front [north] of Fort Jefferson, so as to keep the enemy in check."

On October 23d, Wayne reported from this "strong position," which he named Fort Greenville in honor of his friend in the Revolutionary War, General Nathaniel Greene, that:

"We have recently experienced a little check to one of our convoys which may probably be exaggerated into something serious by the tongue of fame before this reaches you; the following is, however, the fact, viz.: Lieutenant Lowry of the 2d sub-legion and Ensign Boyd of the 1st with a command consisting of ninety non-commissioned officers and privates, having in charge twenty wagons belonging to the quartermaster general's department loaded with grain and one of the contractor's loaded with stores, were attacked early in the morning of the 17th instant about seven miles advanced of Fort St. Clair by a party of Aborigines; those two gallant young gentlemen (who promised at a future day to be ornaments to their profession), together with thirteen non-commissioned officers and privates, bravely fell after an obstinate resistance against superior numbers, being abandoned by the greater part of the escort upon the first discharge. The Savages killed or carried off about seventy horses, leaving the wagons and stores standing in the road, which have all been brought to this camp without any other loss or damage except some trifling articles. . . . It is reported that the Aborigines at Au Glaize [present Defiance, Ohio] have sent their women and children into some secret recess or recesses from their towns; and that the whole of the warriors are collected or collecting in force. . . . A great number of men as well as officers have been left sick and debilitated at the respective garrisons, from a malady called the influenza; among others General Wilkinson has been dangerously ill; he is now at Fort Jefferson and on the recovery. . . .

"The safety of the Western frontiers, the reputation of the legion, the dignity and interest of the nation, all forbid a retrograde manœuvre, or giving up one inch of ground we now possess, until the enemy are compelled to sue for peace."

Wayne's encampment at Greenville was fortified, and part of his army passed the winter there. Major Henry Burbeck, on December 23d, with eight companies of infantry and artillery, was ordered to proceed to the place of General St. Clair's defeat, and there erect a fortification. This stockade enclosure with blockhouses was given the name Fort Recovery; and on the same site its name is perpetuated as that of a thriving village in Mercer County, Ohio.

Observing this steady advance, with fortifications, toward their principal retreats, some of the Aborigines made a movement for peace; and possibly a treaty of peace could have been effected with many of them, but for the ever ready adverse influence of the British. Their desires and continued efforts were "to unite the American Indians" for their own better control of them; which policy Lieutenant-Governor Simcoe expressed at Niagara to the American Peace Commissioners as "the principle of the British government." And these efforts were also continued with the Creeks, Cherokees, and other tribes along the American frontiers south of the Ohio River, thus putting the United States to great expense in men and money for protection there, both before and after this date.

These were troublous years to Americans generally, particularly to those resident west of the Allegheny Mountains. These were beset on all sides, by the British and Savages, and also by the machinations of the French and Spanish, both to involve them in complications with Great Britain, and to again incite the inhabitants of the trans-Allegheny region to a separation from the East.

During these years before railroads, in addition to the remissness of sympathy and protection by

Congress, the natural outlet for the products of the Ohio Basin down the Mississippi River had much to do with the disaffection of the settlers from the East. The statesmen of the East were largely responsible for the beginning of this disaffection of the western settlers, from the want of sympathy in their sufferings, and the expressions and actions that this region was too far distant to be governed by the Atlantic States; also from the opinions that the East could not profit by their trade.

Nor were the States in full accord between themselves. Also the fear of another war with Great Britain was manifest in other ways than the dread of offending this nation by active measures to dispossess it of the vantage possessed in the forts on American soil and in the alliance with the Aborigines. About this time Th. Dwight wrote to Wolcott that: "A war with Great Britain, we, at least in New England, will not enter into. Sooner would ninety-nine out of every hundred of our inhabitants separate from the Union than plunge themselves into an abyss of misery."

The Spanish, French, and British emissaries took advantage of every complication, and circulated their schemes among the settlers from Detroit to Kentucky and the Illinois country. General Wayne well styled this complexity an hydra. At this conjuncture, however, the governmental authorities became vigilant, with good success in several particulars.[1]

The Aborigine chiefs kept in close communication with the British officials, not only with agents Elliott and McKee, but with Detroit and Lieutenant-Governor Simcoe of Niagara; and they even visited Governor-General Lord Dorchester. In an address of welcome to the chiefs February 10, 1794, Lord Dorchester spoke in part as follows:

"Children, since my return I find no appearance of a line [boundary] remains; and from the manner in which the people of the United States push on and act [evidently referring to the Aborigine treaties, and the advance of General Wayne's army] and talk . . . I shall not be surprised if we are at war with them in the course of the present year; and if so a line must be drawn by the warriors. . . . We have acted in the most peaceable manner [sic], and borne the language and conduct of the people of the United States with patience; but I believe our patience is almost exhausted."

[1] *See* President Washington's proclamation of neutrality; Secretary Jefferson's remonstrance regarding the overtures of the Spanish of the Mississippi to the Kentuckians; and against the incitings of the French Minister, Edmond Genest (often written Genêt) to beget sympathy for the French revolutionists against the British and Spanish. Also the American order to reoccupy Fort Massac on the north bank of the Ohio eight miles below the mouth of the Tennessee River, to intercept all illegal transit.

From 1793-1794

This mention of impending war was, evidently, no meaningless talk. Lieutenant-Governor Simcoe was immediately sent to Detroit, he being there February 18th; and a letter from Detroit dated April 17th, reads in part that:

"We have lately had a visit from Governor Simcoe; he came from Niagara through the woods. . . . He has gone to the foot of the [Maumee] Rapids, and three companies of Colonel [Richard] England's regiment have followed him to assist in building a fort there."

This fort, Fort Miami, was a veritable stronghold. It was built on the left bank of the Maumee River (the "Miami of Lake Erie"), near the lower limits of the present village of Maumee, Lucas County, Ohio, which site was then, as now, a great advance into United States territory. Superintendent McKee's British Agency and supply house was about one mile-and-a-half above this fort, and near the lowest rapids of the Maumee—an encroachment of nearly forty miles upon the American soil.

The British also built another fort twelve to fifteen miles within American territory, situated on Turtle Island, just outside of Maumee Bay, twenty miles or more northeast from their Fort Miami. The reinforcements of Wayne's command by Kentucky troops, and all the movements of the army, were regularly reported at this Fort Miami and at Fort Lernoult, Detroit; and, at the advance of General Wayne, Fort Miami was strengthened and further garrisoned, and Major William Campbell of the British Army was sent to replace Captain Caldwell, its first commandant.

President Washington, through Edmund Randolph, Secretary of State, complained to the British Government of Lord Dorchester's address to the Savages, which had been widely circulated among them and the Americans; and he also protested against the building of Fort Miami on American territory. The replies showed that the London Government instigated the aggressions, and offered no relief.

General Wayne reported on July 7, 1794, from his headquarters at Fort Greenville, that:

"At seven o'clock in the morning of the 30th ultimo one of our escorts, consisting of ninety riflemen and fifty dragoons commanded by Major McMahon, was attacked by numerous body of Aborigines under the walls of Fort Recovery, followed by a general assault upon that post and garrison [of about two hundred men] in every direction. The enemy were soon repulsed with great slaughter, but they immediately rallied and reiterated the attack, keeping up a very heavy and constant fire at a more respectable distance for the remainder of the day, which was answered with spirit and effect by the garrison and a part of Major McMahon's command that had regained the post. The Savages were employed during the night [which was foggy and dark] in carrying off their dead by torch light which occasionally drew a fire from the garrison. They, nevertheless, succeeded so well that there were but eight or ten bodies left upon the field, and those close under the range of the guns of the fort.

"The enemy again renewed the attack on the morning of the 1st instant, but were ultimately compelled to retreat with loss and disgrace from that very field where they had upon a former occasion been proudly victorious."

It was apparent that "there were a considerable number of the British and the militia of Detroit mixed with the Savages in the assault," and they expected to find the cannon lost by General St. Clair; but these had been found by the Americans who used them against the assailants. The American loss in the Battle of Fort Recovery was twenty-two killed, thirty wounded, and three missing. Of the horses, fifty-nine were killed, twenty-two wounded, and two hundred and twenty-one were missing; but the General reported that their loss would not in the least retard the advance of the legion after the arrival of the expected mounted volunteers from Kentucky.

The British had again been having communication with the Spanish of the Mississippi, who promised to help them against the Americans.

McKee continued supplying the Savages with the best of firearms (rifles) and other articles of war. Such were used in the attack on Fort Recovery. A party of Delawares and Shawnees afterward showed six American scalps before McKee and addressed him in part as follows:

"We had two actions with Wayne's troops in which a great many of our enemies were killed. Part of their flesh we have brought here with us to convince our friend of the truth of their being now in great force on their march against us; therefore, Father, we desire you to be strong and bid your children make haste to our assistance as was promised."

In further confirmation of the aggressive action of the British, and of their apprehension that the Americans would retaliate to their harm, the following letters from Colonel Alexander McKee, British Agent to the Aborigines, written to Colonel Richard England, Commandant at Detroit, are given, they being endorsed, "On His Majesty's Service," viz.:

"[Foot of the Maumee] Rapids,
"July 5, 1794.

"Sir: I send this by a party of Saganas [Saginaw Aborigines] who returned yesterday from Fort

Recovery where the whole body of Indians, except the Delawares who had gone another route, imprudently attacked the fort on Monday the 30th of last month, and lost 16 or 17 men besides a good many wounded.

"Everything had been settled prior to their leaving the fallen timber [about four miles above foot of the rapids] and it had been agreed upon to confine themselves to taking convoys and attacking at a distance from the forts, if they should have the address to entice the enemy [Americans] out; but the impetuosity of the Mackinac Indians and their eagerness to begin the nearest, prevailed with the others to alter their system, the consequences of which from the present appearance of things may most materially injure the interests of these people. Both the Mackinac and Lake Indians seemed resolved on going home again, having completed the belts they carried with scalps and prisoners, and having no provisions there at the Glaize [the present Defiance, Ohio] to subsist upon, so that his Majesty's posts will derive no security from the late great influx of Indians into this part of the country, should they persist in their resolution of returning so soon.

"The immediate object of the attack was three hundred packhorses going from this fort [Recovery] to Fort Greenville, in which the Indians completely succeeded, taking and killing all of them. But the commanding officer, Captain Gibson, sending out a troop of cavalry, and bringing his infantry out in front of his post, the Indians attacked him and killed about fifty, among whom is Captain Gibson and two other officers. On the near approach of the Indians to the fort, the remains of his garrison retired into it, and from their loopholes killed and wounded as already mentioned. Captain Elliott writes that they are immediately to hold a council at the Glaize [Auglaize or Grand Glaise, as above] in order to try if they can prevail upon the Lake Indians to remain; but without provisions, ammunition, &c., being sent to that place, I conceive it will be extremely difficult to keep them together.

"With great respect, I have the honor to be
"Your obedient and humble servant,
"A. McKee."

Great efforts were again made by the British, not only to keep together the Savages already near "their posts," but to have those "who had gone another route" return to them. Another letter from McKee to Colonel England reads as follows:

"Rapids, August 13, 1794.

"Sir: I was honored last night with your letter of the 11th, and was extremely glad to find you are making such exertions to supply the Indians with provisions.

"Captain Elliott arrived yesterday; what he has brought will greatly relieve us, having been obliged yesterday to take all the corn and flour which the traders had here.

"A scouting party from the Americans carried off a man and a woman yesterday morning between this place and Roche de Bout, and afterwards attacked a small party of Delawares in their camp; but they were repulsed with the loss of a man, whom they either hid or threw into the river. They killed

a Delaware woman. Scouts are sent up to view the situation of the army; and we now muster 1000 Indians. All the Lake Indians from Sagina downwards should not lose one moment in joining their brethren, as every accession of strength is an addition to their spirits. I have the honor to be, &c.
"A. McKee."

The testimony of Savages of different tribes, taken by General Wayne, and others, yet further confirms the influence of the British in promoting, and fomenting, the war, even after most of the tribes desired peace with the Americans.

CHAPTER IX

WAYNE'S ARMY DEFEATS A HYDRA OF CONSPIRACIES

Further Advance of Wayne's Army—A Most Momentous Campaign—Builds Forts Adams and Defiance—The Enemy Flees—Wayne's Last Overture for Peace—The Army Nears the Enemy—Builds Fort Deposit, and Advances to Complete Victory—Buildings and Crops of British and their Allies Destroyed—Wayne's Emphatic Letters to the Commandant of Fort Miami—The Casualties—Army Returns and Strengthens Fort Defiance—The Red Savages—British Strengthen their Forts in United States Territory.

MAJOR-GENERAL CHARLES SCOTT, with about sixteen hundred volunteer cavalrymen from Kentucky, who had been sent home for the winter, rejoined General Wayne's army, then numbering possibly two thousand soldiers, at Fort Greenville July 26, 1794; and the next day General Wayne ordered the general advance movement for the 28th.

This was to be a most momentous campaign.

If this, the third army against these "allied" foes, be defeated, the country west and southwest of the Allegheny Mountains would, evidently, thenceforth be completely dominated by the British, and completely lost to the Americans, unless a general war was declared with Great Britain.

The army took up its march on the morning named in General Order, and soon evidences of the enemies' scouts became apparent. It was necessary to make a road through the great forest, composed of great trees of oak, beech, maple, etc., which were larger and more numerous as the army advanced. The deep Beaver Swamp had to be bridged with "infinite" labor. At the crossing of the River St. Mary, a stop of two days was made for the purpose of building a fort, which was named Fort Adams. Here General Wayne was caught under a falling tree while urging more haste upon the choppers of logs for blockhouses and palisades. This accident "nearly put an end to his existence" but his indomitable will power forced him, and his army, forward without delay, and against all obstacles.

On August 8, 1794, the army arrived at its "Camp Grand Oglaize" (junction of the Auglaize River with the Maumee, site of the present city of Defiance, Ohio) at half-past ten o'clock in the morning. Here Wayne and his army were delighted with the beauty and fertility of the region. His diarist wrote that:

"This place far excels in beauty any in the western country, and believed equalled by none in the Atlantic States. Here are vegetables of every kind in abundance; and we have marched four or five miles in corn fields down the Oglaize [Auglaize], and there are not less than one thousand acres of corn round the town."

This being the point of confluence of three rivers, the Auglaize and Bean (later named the Tiffin) with the Maumee, it was naturally a great gathering place for the Aborigines; and but the evening before the arrival of the army a large number of them fled down the Maumee, and their straggling huts were found abandoned. This fact General Wayne attributed to their being informed regarding the details of his army by a deserter from his ranks a few days before; and the General considered it a favorable circumstance. He had feinted toward the Miami villages at the head of the Maumee, and then as he thought toward Roche de Bout, then followed down the left bank of the Auglaize River "in a central direction"; and he congratulated himself, as well as the Secretary of War, that he had "gained possession of the grand emporium of the hostile Aborigines of the West without loss of blood." Hereabout, as well as elsewhere along the rivers, the British had encouraged the women of the Savages to cultivate corn and vegetables to relieve as much as possible the demands of the Savages on the British food supplies.

The army remained at the mouth of the Auglaize River about one week. During this time there was here built, with Wayne's characteristic energy, a strong fort which he named Fort Defiance, a place where he could defy the red Savages and their British allies.

He not only planned and superintended the building of this fort, but from the first day of his arrival he continued his efforts to win over the Savages to peace with the United States, sending to them by "special flag" a well prepared letter which he styled his last overture for peace. He told the warriors addressed that he held the several Aborigines, who had been captured by his scouts, as hostages for the safe return of his "special flag." The bearer of this was Christopher Miller, who had lived with the Aborigines several years, and had been captured from them six months before being chosen to bear this flag.

General Wayne felt confident of success in the event of a conflict with the enemy. The day before starting from Fort Defiance to meet whoever opposed him, he wrote to the Secretary of War reporting the situation of the enemies, and added: "Should war be their choice, that blood be upon their own heads. America shall no longer be insulted with impunity. To an all powerful and just God I therefore commit myself and gallant army."

On August 15th, leaving a garrison of about one hundred soldiers to guard, and to continue work on, Fort Defiance, as had also been done at the other forts, the army marched about forty-four miles down the left bank of the Maumee River toward the Fallen Timber, a place chosen by the enemies to make their stand against the oncoming Americans.

On the 18th, Wayne and his army arrived opposite Roche de Bout, a narrow mass of sectile limestone that had been left in the river in wearing its channel, and which had been a landmark for the French for over one hundred years. Upon the high, precipitous left bank, the General planned an encampment within which the soldiers "threw up works to secure and deposit the heavy baggage of the troops, so that the men might be light for action, provided the enemy have presumption to favor us with an interview, which if they should think proper to do, the troops are in such high spirits that we will make an easy victory of them."

At five o'clock in the morning of August 20th, 1794, the army marched from Fort Deposit down the left bank of the Maumee and, about three miles distant, met the enemy in Fallen Timber (the result of a former tornado) on and around Presque Isle, a prominence on the river bank, a former island in the river's early geologic history and another landmark of the early French. The enemy was here hidden in the grass and behind the fallen trees, and the unexpected discharge of their guns into the ranks at short range threw Wayne's advance guard into confusion; but the army was prepared for this and there was an immediate rally with definite orders from the General, who at once saw the condition of affairs. The quickly ordered "charge with trailed arms" routed the Savages from their ambush and the rapid attack and slaughter of them in front and flank soon caused their general and promiscuous flight, with the Americans in such rapid and close pursuit for three or four miles, even to within range of the British Fort Miami's guns, that only part of Wayne's command could participate. General Wayne reported that:

"From every account the enemy amounted to two thousand combatants. The troops actually engaged against them were short of nine hundred . . . with loss of thirty-three killed and one hundred wounded [eleven of whom died before this report was written]. The loss of the enemy, composed of Aborigines, Canadian militia, and volunteers, was more than double to that of the Federal army. The woods were strewed for a considerable distance with dead bodies of the Aborigines and their white auxiliaries."

On his march down the river, about sixteen miles below Fort Defiance, General Wayne was met by Christopher Miller, his "special flag," on his return from the enemy. The reply to the General's "last overture for peace" was, "If you will remain at Grand Oglaize [Fort Defiance] ten days we will let you know whether we will be for peace or war." It was fortunate for the Canadian British that General Wayne did not mind this reply. August 18th, two days before the Battle of Fallen Timber, Lieutenant-Governor and Colonel Simcoe wrote to Governor-General Lord Dorchester that he "would go to Detroit with all the force he could muster." Simcoe was pronounced in his hope that this third large American army would meet the fate of the other two. General Wayne's report shows that reinforcements of the enemy were received two days before, and later reports show reinforcement a few days after, the battle. His report to the Secretary of War further reads as follows:

"The Americans remained three days and nights on the banks of the Maumee in front of the field of battle, during which time all the houses and cornfields were consumed and destroyed for a considerable distance, both above and below Fort Miami, as well as within pistol shot of that garrison, who were compelled to remain tacit spectators to this general devastation and conflagration, among which were the houses, stores and property of Colonel McKee the British Aborigine agent and principal stimulator of the war now existing between the United States and the Savages."

Major William Campbell of the British 24th Regiment, who was commanding officer of Fort Miami, early addressed a note to General Wayne protesting against his near approach to "a post belonging to his Majesty the King of Great Britain, occupied by his Majesty's troops," declaring that he "knew of no war existing between Great Britain and America." This gave occasion for two sharp letters from General Wayne, ordering the Major to get out of American territory with his command, Wayne knowing of course that an officer must obey only the orders of his commanding officer; but he chafed under this restraint, and reported to the Secretary of War, regarding Major Campbell's third courteous but firm letter, that:

"The only notice taken of this letter, was by immediately setting fire to, and destroying, everything within view of the fort, and even under the muzzles of his guns. Had Mr. Campbell carried his threats into execution, it is more than probable that he would have experienced a storm."

Prisoners were captured at the Battle of Fallen Timber, British soldiers and subjects, as well as their allies, the Savages, and they gave much important information and evidence.

The army arrived at Fort Defiance, on its return, August 27th. The same fortifying of Wayne's camps was continued, to a moderate degree, as had been done with his advance, he always being on the guard against surprise by the stealthy foe. This gave rise to the statement by the Savages that General Wayne "never slept." The rapidity and security of his army's movements through "their country" caused them to call him "the wind"; and his impetuous, and to them disastrous, charge and pursuit at the Battle of Fallen Timber gave him the name of "whirlwind" by their survivors.

Near the close of Wayne's report after his return to Fort Defiance, he wrote in part as follows:

"It is, however, not improbable that the enemy may make one desperate effort against this army, as it is said that a reinforcement was hourly expected at Fort Miami from Niagara as well as numerous tribes of Aborigines living on the margin and islands of the lakes. This is a business rather to be wished for rather than dreaded whilst the army remains in force. Their numbers will only tend to confuse the Savages and the victory will be the more complete and decisive, and which may eventually ensure a permanent and happy peace."

Attention was at once given to the strengthening of Fort Defiance by the army, and the gathering of the corn and vegetables growing within comfortable distance. The walls and roofs of the four blockhouses, and the palisades, were made "bomb proof"; a broad water-moat was made, with glacis nearly surrounding, and fascines with pickets. The junction of the Auglaize with the Maumee River was approached by an underground passageway for a safe and unlimited supply of water. This was the strongest fortification built by Wayne.

Immediately following the Battle of Fallen Timber, many of the Savages, not finding the expected support and protection from the British Fort Miami, fled to Detroit, the British headquarters, where an estimate placed their number, within a few days, at thirteen hundred. Additional evidence of the severe effect of the battle on them and the British militia with them there, was the equipment, at Detroit, of another hospital with an additional surgeon, the expense of which was approved by Lieutenant-Governor Simcoe October 31st.

The British also proceeded at once to strengthen Fort Lernoult at Detroit; and a blockhouse was built on the opposite side of the river; also six gunboats were constructed for patrolling the river and communicating with Forts Turtle Island and Miami.

As fast as possible Colonel McKee assembled the Savages by the Maumee River at the mouth of Swan Creek, about eight miles below Fort Miami. The autumn and the following winter were times of great suffering among them. Their crops having been destroyed by the army, rendered them more than ever dependent on the British who, not being prepared for so great a task, and withal quite fatigued before with their exactions, "did not half supply them." They were huddled so closely together along the Maumee that much sickness prevailed from want of sanitary regulations, exposure, and scant food supply, in addition to the malaria of the warmer weather, stored in their systems. The few domestic animals they possessed also languished, died, or were killed, and were eaten by their masters. They became impatient, murmured at the failure of the British to protect and supply them according to promise, and lamented that they had not made peace with the Americans.

The British also suffered severely during this time. Colonel Richard England wrote, October 28, 1794, to Francis Le Maître, British Military Secretary, complaining of the great amount of food supplies taken by Colonel McKee (to the Maumee River at the mouth of Swan Creek) for the Aborigines; also for those taken "for the garrisons at Fort Miamies [about thirty-five miles within American territory] and at Turtles Island" (at the mouth of Maumee Bay). He paid the soldiers of these garrisons "a dollar a chord for Cutting & piling the Fire wood necessary for these Posts for the winter." Loss by death at these posts "by that unfavorable climate" was very severe. At the date of Colonel England's writing there were:

"of the 24th Regiment only one hundred & fifty-four on the Surgeon's sick list Report. Those who survive will not I fear be fit for any Duty this winter, as their disorder is of such a nature as to give but little hope of a speedy or permanent recovery.

Every attention is paid to them that this [Detroit] Post will admit of, but from the very unusual Consumption of Medicine, Our Stock, as well as all that could be purchased here, is totally Expended, and we look with impatience for a supply from Lower Canada."

CHAPTER X

THE TAMING OF THE BROKEN SAVAGE SPIRIT

Wayne Marches his Army to the Site of the Miami Villages—There Builds Fort Wayne—Receives and Makes Valuable Friends of Deserters from the British—Disaffection of Kentucky Volunteers—They are Sent Home—Savage Scouts Active at Fort Defiance—Wayne's Suggestion of General Council with Aborigines Meets Favor.

GENERAL WAYNE and army remained at Fort Defiance until September 14, 1794, nursing the wounded, sick, and fatigued, working about the fort, disciplining his army, gathering the crops, and despatching detachments for other needed supplies. These detachments were delayed by bad condition of trails, bad weather, and malarial affections; and the troops on varied duties also suffered with ague and allied affections. A few thoughtless ones strayed beyond the officers' orders, and were killed or captured by prowling Savages.

Fort Defiance being completed, well garrisoned,

and supplied, and everything being in readiness, the army took up the line of march in the morning of September 14th, crossed to the left (north) bank of the Maumee, and moved westward, the destination being the site of the Miami villages at the head of the river, the place of General Harmar's sad defeat four years previous. Arrival there was made toward evening of the 17th, without molestation or very serious experience.

The next day, the General selected the site for, and planned, a fort, which the army built as soon as the now wet and windy weather would permit.

Four deserters from the British arrived the 23d, and gave valuable information. This was the second lot of four who arrived this week. On the 26th, one of the army's scouts reported that the Savages had been troublesome at Fort Defiance, killing some of the garrison under its walls.

The work on the new fort progressed well for a time; then the volunteers from Kentucky lost patience with work and started to disobey the orders of their General, Scott. He, however, was equal to the occasion, telling them that "if they made the smallest delay they should lose all their pay and be reported to the war office as revolters." For a short time this had the desired effect upon them; and the entire army was improved in obedi ence therefrom. The diary for next day, October 3d, reads that "Every officer, non-commissioned officer, and soldier belonging to the square are on fatigue this day, hauling trees on the hind wheels of wagons." Again on the 7th, "The volunteers are soon tired of work and have refused to labor any longer; they have stolen and killed seventeen beeves in the course of these two days past." In consequence, all the soldiers were necessarily confined to half rations for some days.

General Wayne continued active with Canadian deserters from the British, and the reports brought to him by them. He found opportunity to win their aid toward furthering the American cause; for, by giving them pardon, and some pecuniary profit for supplying the American garrisons, he won their influence in diverting the American Savages from the British to the Americans, their rightful advisers. These deserters well performed their part of the contract, and the result again showed the wisdom of President Washington's choice of a commander for this very important kind of work, as well as for discipline and battle.

On October 12th, the mounted volunteers from Kentucky were started for Fort Greenville, to be mustered and dismissed; and six days later other detachments moved away for special work. The next day, Sunday, the troops remaining at the head of the river were not ordered to work, it being the first day of rest for four weeks; and they were gathered for divine service.

On the 22d, the command of the new fort was given to Lieutenant-Colonel Hamtramck, with five companies of infantry and one company of artillery. The troops were paraded; he ordered the "firing fifteen rounds of cannon," one for each State then composing the Union, and gave the new post the name Fort Wayne. This fort was destined to be the most enduring of all General Wayne's fortifications, lasting twenty-four years. While not so compact and strong for defence as Fort Defiance, it was to become a very important post for the completion of its builder's work in subjugating the Savages, so well begun; and a place for acting an important part in a later war against the continued aggressions of the British and their savage allies. Its name and site, as those of Fort Defiance, have been perpetuated in a beautiful, flourishing, and patriotic city.

Leaving Fort Wayne and the appointed garrison in good condition, the remainder of Wayne's army resumed its march October 28, 1794, passing up the right bank of the St. Marys River, past Fort Adams, to the site of the present city of St. Marys, where Wayne afterwards built a fort, and thence southward. They arrived at Fort Greenville November 2, 1794, receiving from there a salute of "twenty-four rounds from a six-pounder."

General Wayne could not remain idle; nor would he permit his soldiers to remain idle. His grasp of the situation was complete, and his views of its necessities were practical. His first duty was to keep his trains of packhorses on the trail, along the great number of long, weary miles through the wilderness, going for, and returning with, supplies for his army and for his several forts.

The situation also required more fortifications, and protected camping places for the supply trains. In person, he carefully selected the sites, and planned, and directed his soldiers to build, Forts Piqua and Loramie by the upper waters of the Miami River (flowing southward into the Ohio); Fort St. Mary, by the river with the same name, the southern tributary of the Maumee River, and Fort Auglaize, by the "head of the Auglaize." This was the head of its navigation, at the north end of the portage from Fort St. Mary to the Auglaize River, and thus communicated directly with Fort Defiance by a shorter and better way than his first trail. The sites of these forts, like those of all other forts built by this wide-awake General, were well chosen; and larger fortifications were there built for the War of 1812, as shown on later pages.

The Secretary of War was kept informed, by full reports, regarding these works, and of the General's activities in diplomatically bringing about further changes in the minds of the Aborigines regarding their best interests. This work began soon after the Battle of Fallen Timber.

George Ironside, an observing and honest Englishman and former prominent British trader among the Aborigines at the junction of the Auglaize with the Maumee River, where Wayne later built Fort Defiance, also gave aid to this work by writing and saying that, at the Battle of Fallen Timber, "The Aborigines as yet had felt only the weight of General Wayne's little finger, and that he would surely destroy all the tribes if they did not turn to peace with the Americans."

Some Frenchmen, British soldiers captured in Wayne's great battle, and also later deserters from the British, were soon won over to Wayne by his strong personality, and to the American cause by its reasonableness; and they became willing and valuable agents in approaching and converting the Aborigines in the time of their great distress in the winter of 1794-95, following the destruction of their crops, and the neglect of them by their allies, the British. On invitation, chiefs visited the American fortifications, and General Wayne at Greenville, where their temporary wants were supplied; and a grand council of them with the Americans was suggested. This suggestion was well received by the visiting chiefs, and they were instructed to communicate this request to others.

General Wayne's Reports to the Secretary of War contain much valuable information. That of December 23, 1794, reads in part as follows:

"I have the honor to inform you that the flag from the Wyandots of Sandusky, after an absence of forty-two days, returned to Greenville on the evening of the 14th instant.

"The enclosed copies of letters and speeches will best demonstrate the insidious part recently taken by the British agents, Messrs. Simcoe, McKee and Brant, to stimulate the savages to continue the war, who, being too well acquainted with the near approach of that period in which the legion [Wayne's army] will be dissolved, have artfully suggested a suspension of hostilities until spring, in order to lull us into a state of security to prevent the raising of troops, and to afford the Aborigines an opportunity to make their fall and winter hunt unmolested.

"In the interim the British are vigilantly employed in strengthening and making additions to their fortification at the foot of the rapids of the Miamies of the Lake [Maumee River] evidently with a view of convincing the Aborigines of their determination to assist and protect them; hence there is strong ground to conclude that Governor Simcoe has not received any orders to the contrary, otherwise he would not presume to persevere in those nefarious acts of hostility.

"The Wyandots and other Aborigines at and in the vicinity of the rapids of Sandusky River, are completely within our power, and their hunting grounds all within striking distance; hence their present solicitude for a suspension of hostilities.

"But unless Congress has already, or will immediately adopt effectual measures to raise troops to garrison this as well as the other posts already established, it would only be a work of supererogation, as the whole must otherwise be abandoned by the middle of May. I have, however, succeeded in dividing and distracting the counsels of the hostile Aborigines, and hope through that means eventually to bring about a general peace, or to compel the refractory to pass the Mississippi and to the northwest side of the lakes.

"The British agents have greatly the advantage in this business at present by having it in their power to furnish the Aborigines with every necessary supply of arms, ammunition, and clothing, in exchange for their skins and furs, which will always make the Savages dependent upon them until the United States establish trading houses in their country, from which they can be supplied with equal facility, and at reasonable rates."

This suggestion of trading posts for the Aborigines, a measure that should have been put in execution years before, was later adopted by the United States; but, by that time, the British had circumvented the good the system should have done both to the Aborigines and to the United States.

Wayne's work to draw the Aborigines away from the British influence was not of an easy character, nor were his strong and prudent efforts attended with constant success. As he stated, the British had the advantage; in fact they had several advantages; and McKee rallied the authorities to renewed activities. McKee, in a letter of March 27, 1795, to Joseph Chew, Secretary of the British Aborigine Office, chided the government for leaving to shift for themselves "the poor Indians who have long fought for us, and bled freely for us, which is no bar to a peaceable accommodation with America."

The British had several times before, during the Revolutionary War, met General Wayne under conditions in their favor, and had found in him an opponent whose prowess was worthy of their best efforts. This contest against them and their savage allies, destined to be his last great work for his country, was yet to show the enemies that this typical American soldier had lost none of his patriotism, alertness, and wisdom; characteristics which had shed a lustre on American arms that will never fade.

CHAPTER XI

THE MOST IMPORTANT OF ALL TREATIES WITH THE SAVAGES

Discipline in the Army—Wayne's Diplomacy in Winning the Savages to Peace—His Agents in the Work—Exchange of Prisoners—The Treaty of Greenville, August 3, 1795—Number of Tribes in the Agreement.

NOTWITHSTANDING the great victories of the armies and navies of the United Colonies and States of America, peace has had victories greater than war throughout this nation's history; and her forbearance toward offenders, and her magnanimity toward the conquered, have been examples to all nations which have added greatly to the peace and civilization of all other peoples; and these great principles of humanity will continue to increase in power therefrom throughout the world.

The victories of General Wayne's army were signal in this campaign through the wilderness far from the base of supplies; but his victory for the peace, soon to follow, opened up the way to conquer, without further shedding of blood, all of the Savages and, also, for a time, their allies the British.

General Wayne was a good judge of men. His choice of Colonel John Francis Hamtramck as commandant of Fort Wayne was well considered and appropriate. This site of the noted "Miami Villages" had been the headquarters of the Miamis and other strong tribes of Savages for generations; and hence, for many years, had emanated numerous raiding and murdering parties of Savages against the American frontiers. Colonel Hamtramck was a small Canadian Frenchman, who had been many years in the American service, and, always having proved himself patriotic, capable, and meritorious, had been advanced accordingly. His letter-book, which was in part saved from destruction in Detroit after his death, sheds some sidelights on the character of his soldiers, the government's orders for discipline at that time, and the work of winning the Savages to peace. Hamtramck's reports were all addressed from Fort Wayne to General Wayne at Greenville, and some of them are in part as follows, the first under date December 5, 1794:

"It is with a great degree of mortification that I am obliged to inform Your Excellency of the great propensity many of the soldiers have for larceny. I have flogged them until I am tired. The economic allowance of one hundred lashes, allowed by government, does not appear a sufficient inducement for a rascal to act the part of an honest man. I have now a number in confinement and in irons for having stolen four quarters of beef on the night of the 3d instant. I could wish them to be tried by a general court martial, in order to make an example of some of them. I shall keep them confined until the pleasure of your excellency is known."

The General had a better way of dealing with his men than flogging them—a way that appealed to their thoughtful and better judgment for the control of their excesses, and for the proper obedience of all the orders of their officers, so necessary for soldiers and the cause they represent; when so far in the wilderness particularly. He held the confidence and respect of his men, and they quickly responded to his every wish; otherwise he could not have swept through this dense and difficult "black swamp" the way he had done, and so quickly crushed all opposition of the enemies in the great battle by the Maumee.

Colonel Hamtramck's letters continue, with date December 29th:

"Yesterday a number of chiefs of the Chippeways, Ottawas, Socks [Sacs] and Potawotamies arrived here with the two Lassells deserters from the British.

It appears that the Shawanese, Delawares, and Miamies remain still under the influence of McKee; but Lassell thinks that they will be compelled to come into the measures of the other Aborigines. After the chiefs have rested a day or two, I will send them to headquarters.

"December 29th: . . . Since my letter to Your Excellency of the present date, two war-chiefs have arrived from the Miami nation, and inform me that their nation will be here in a few days, from whence they will proceed to Greenville. They also bring intelligence of the remaining tribes of savages acceding to the prevalent wish for peace, and collecting for the purpose the chiefs of their nations, who, it is expected, will make their appearance at this post about the same time the Miamies may come forward.

"January 15, 1795: . . . A number of chiefs and warriors of the Miamis arrived at the garrison on the 13th instant. Having informed them that I could do nothing with them, and that it was necessary for them to proceed to headquarters, finding it inconvenient for so many to go, they selected five who are going under charge of Lieutenant Massie, and perhaps will be accompanied by some warriors. The one whose name is Jean Baptiste Richardville, is half white and a village chief of the nation.

"As you are well acquainted with the original cause of the war with the Aborigines, I shall not say much upon it, except to observe that all the French traders, who were so many machines to the British agents, can be bought, and McKee, being then destitute of his satellites, will remain *solus*, with perhaps his few Shawanese, to make penance for his past iniquities.

"Since writing the foregoing, I have had a talk with the chiefs. I have shown them the necessity of withdrawing themselves from the headquarters of corruption, and invited them to come and take possession of their former habitations [across the Maumee and St. Mary rivers from the garrison of Fort Wayne] which they have promised me to do. Richardville tells me, that as soon as he returns he will go on the Salamonie [River] on [near] the head of the Wabash, and there make a village. He has also promised me to open the navigation of the Wabash to the flag of the United States.

"February 3rd: . . . Lieutenant Massey arrived on the 31st. The Indians also returned on the 29th in high spirits and very much pleased with their reception by you [General Wayne] at headquarters. They assure me that they will absolutely make a lasting peace with the United States.

"March 1st: . . . I have now with me about forty Indians on a visit. They are Potawotamies, who live on Bear Creek [in the present Lenawee County, Michigan]. They say that as they are making peace with us, they will expect us to give them some corn to plant next spring. Indeed all the Aborigines who have been here have requested that I would inform Your Excellency of their miserable situation, and that they expect everything from you.

"March 5: . . . A number of Potawotamie Indians arrived here yesterday from Huron River, Michigan. They informed me that they were sent by their nation at that place, and by the Ottawas and Chippeways living on the same river, as also in the name of the Chippeways living on the Saginaw River which empties into Lake Huron, in order to join in the good intention of the other Aborigines, by establishing a permanent peace with the United States. I informed them that I was not the first chief, and invited them to go to Greenville; to which they replied that it was rather a long journey, but from the great desire they had to see the Wind (for they called you so) they would go. I asked them for an explication of your name. They told me that on the 20th August last, you were exactly like a whirlwind, which drives and tears everything before it. Mr. LeChauvre, a Frenchman, is a trader with them and has come as their interpreter. Father Burke continues his exhortations. He assures the inhabitants that if any of them should be so destitute of every principle of honor and religion as to aid or advise the Indians to come to the Americans, they shall be anathematized. He is now a commissary and issues corn to the Aborigines. Mr. LeChauvre informs me that Burke is going, in the spring, to Michilimackinac. Of consequence we may easily judge of his mission. He will, no doubt, try to stop the nations from coming in to the treaty. How would it do to take him prisoner? I think that it could be done very easily.

"March 17: . . . I had very great hopes that the man who deserted when on his post would have been made an example of; but weakness too often appears in the shape of lenity, for he was only sentenced to receive one hundred lashes, to be branded, and drummed out. This man, from his past conduct, was perfectly entitled to the gallows."[1]

[1] For additional letters from Colonel Hamtramck to General Wayne regarding the winning of the Aborigines to peace, see Slocum's *History of the Maumee River Basin.*

The diplomacy and persistency of General Wayne and his agents were successful and January 1, 1795, he sent a message to the petitioning Wyandots at Sandusky that the chiefs of the Chippewas, Ottawas, Sacs, Pottawotamis, and Miamis had arrived at Fort Wayne and would soon visit him at Greenville in the interest of peace.

On January 24th, he reported to the Secretary of War that two preliminary articles of peace had been signed by him and the sachems and war chiefs of the Chippewas, Pottawotamis, Sacs, and Miamis. These preliminary articles provided that hostilities should cease; that there should be a meeting for council and treaty at Fort Greenville on or about June 15, 1795; that immediate information should be given to General Wayne of all hostile movements that came to the knowledge of any of the Aborigines; and that the General was to reciprocate in their interest.

Soon after this date, the Delawares visited Fort Defiance and exchanged prisoners to the number of nine, this being all of the Aborigines then held at that place. John Brickell, from whom this information was obtained, then fourteen years of age, had been captive with the Delawares four years, and on this occasion keenly felt the want of another Aborigine prisoner with the garrison, that he also might be exchanged to return to his kinsfolk. In May, however, the Delawares again appeared across the Maumee River from Fort Defiance and discharged their guns in salute. The garrison of the fort returned the salute with a cannon shot for each State then in the Union. At this visit Brickell was surrendered to the garrison with some sentiment on the part of the Aborigines, and good fellowship prevailed.

Wayne early prepared for the prospective large meeting of the Aborigines at Greenville for council, and for a treaty of peace. Ground was cleared, an ample Council House was soon built by his experienced axemen that would protect from the sun or rain and yet be open at the sides for free ventilation. A large quantity of clothing and other useful articles for presents, and bountiful supplies of food, had been ordered from the East, and all were received in good time.

About the 1st of June a goodly number of Delaware, Ottawa, Pottawotami, and Eel River Aborigines began to arrive, and all were well received. Others arrived each day, and, June 16th, the General Council was opened, with good attendance. After smoking the Calumet of Peace, an oath of accuracy and fidelity was subscribed to by eight interpreters, and by Henry De Butts as secretary.

As presiding officer General Wayne stated the object of the Council, exhibited his commission received from President Washington, and put all present in good humor by his happy remarks, saying, in closing, "The heavens are bright, the roads are open; we will rest in peace and love, and wait the arrival of our brothers [referring to the tardy Aborigines who, at similar times, like sulky children desired to be sent for with special overtures]. We will on this happy occasion be merry without, however, passing the bounds of temperance and sobriety."

Frequent arrivals of large numbers continued. The third day of July all were called together, and the General gave them their first lesson in American patriotism. He explained to them why all the States of the American Union celebrated the Fourth of July each year, adding:

"To-morrow we shall for the twentieth time salute the return of this happy anniversary, rendered still more dear by the brotherly union of the Americans and red people; to-morrow all the people within these lines will rejoice; you, my brothers, shall also rejoice in your respective encampments. I called you together to explain these matters to you; do not, therefore, be alarmed at the report of our big guns; they will do you no harm; they will be the harbingers of peace and gladness, and their roar will ascend into the heavens. The flag of the United States, and the colors of this legion, shall be given to the wind to be fanned by its gentlest breeze in honor of the birthday of American freedom. I will now show you our colors that you may know them to-morrow. Formerly they were displayed as ensigns of war and battle; now they will be exhibited as emblems of peace and happiness. This eagle which you now see, holds close his bunch of arrows whilst he seems to stretch forth, as a more valuable offering, the inestimable branch of peace. The Great Spirit seems disposed to incline us all to repose for the future under its grateful shade and wisely enjoy the blessings which attend it."

Aborigines continued to arrive. On July 18th, a sachem, arriving with a band of Chippewas, said to the General, "We would have come in greater numbers but for Brant's endeavors to prevent us in interest of the British."

With great thoughtfulness and circumspection, the text of the treaty had been drawn, and the General, by his cheerful yet serious and dignified demeanor, impressed all present to a careful consideration and assent to each of its provisions, separately. Notwithstanding the continued arrival of Aborigines, the business of the Council was continued day by day until its completion.

The Report to the Secretary of War, August 9, 1795, reads in part as follows:

"It is with infinite pleasure I now inform you that

From 1794-1795

a treaty of peace between the United States of America and all the late hostile tribes of Indians Northwest of the Ohio River, was unanimously and voluntarily agreed to, and cheerfully signed, by all the sachems and war chiefs of the respective nations on the 3rd, and exchanged on the 7th instant."

The number of Aborigines, and of tribes and bands, credited with being at the treaty, including very late arrivals, were:

Tribes.	Number.	Sworn Interpreters.
Wyandots	180	Isaac Zane and Abraham Williams.
Delawares	381	Cabot Wilson.
Shawnees	143	Jacques Lasselle and Christopher Miller.
Ottawas	45	M. Morans and Bt. Sans Crainte.
Chippewas	46	
Pottawotamis	240	
Miamis and Eel Rivers	73	William Wells.
Weas and Piankishaws	12	
Kickapoos and Kaskaskias	10	
Total, Twelve	1130	Eight.

A number of hostile Cherokees, who were lingering around the headwaters of the Scioto River, did not accept the invitations to the Council; and on August 3d the General notified them of the treaty with all the other tribes, also of the treaty recently effected with their brethren in the South. He also notified them to accept immediately his last invitation to come to Greenville and enter into articles of peace or they would stand alone and unprotected. Some of them accompanied "Captain Longhair," a principal Cherokee chief, and the messenger, to Fort Greenville, and soon thereafter accompanied the chief to their former home in the South. The others promised to hunt quietly along the Scioto River until their crops ripened, when they would return South to remain.

The Aborigines were loth to leave Greenville, even after the General's eloquent farewell speech. Each of the more prominent chiefs desired to have the last word with the great warrior who had now pleased them exceedingly.

Buckongehelas, the great chief of the Delawares, seemed to voice the sentiments of all when he said, in free and rounded translation:

"Your children all well understand the sense of the treaty which is now concluded. We experience daily proofs of your increasing kindness. I hope we all may have sense enough to enjoy our dawning happiness. Many of your people are yet among us. I trust they will be immediately restored. Last winter our King [Tetebokshke] came forward to you with two, and when he returned with your speech to us, we immediately prepared to come forward with the remainder, which we delivered at Fort Defiance. All who know me, know me to be a man and a warrior, and I now declare that I will for the future be as true and steady a friend to the United States as I have heretofore been an active enemy. We have one bad man among us who, a few days ago, stole three of your horses; two of them shall this day be returned to you, and I hope I shall be able to prevent that young man doing any more mischief to our Father the Fifteen Fires [States]."

On September 9th between sixty and seventy refractory and hostile Shawnee warriors, led by Chief Pucksekaw or Jumper, arrived at Fort Greenville and wished to be included in the treaty. From the efforts of Chief Blue Jacket, they brought and surrendered four American captives, three of whom were taken in Randolph County, Virginia, July 13th of this year (1795).

These being the last of the hostiles, General Wayne turned his attention to affairs best calculated to make the treaty, and peace, permanent.

CHAPTER XII

THE WEST GAINS POSSESSION OF PART OF ITS RIGHTS

Treaty with Spain Favorable to the West—Abandonment of Forts—British again Endeavor to Seduce the Aborigines of the United States—The Jay Treaty Favorable to the West—British Surrender American Forts—Death of General Wayne—Wayne County Organized—More French and Spanish Plots—Separation of the West from the East again Suggested—British Threaten Spanish Possessions in the South.

THE United States concluded a treaty of friendship, of limits, and of navigation with Spain, October 27, 1795. This treaty further allayed for a time the feeling of anxiety and unrest with some, of ambition with others, and contributed to the strengthening of the bond of union between the West and the East. This was also a year of much migration from the East, with increase of settlements along the rivers of southern Ohio, other southern parts of the Northwest Territory, and south of the Ohio River.

From 1795-1798

In January, 1796, General Wayne visited the seat of general government, General James Wilkinson being given chief command of the Northwestern Army during his absence. Great courtesy and deference were shown Wayne upon his arrival in Philadelphia, and also upon his visit to his native county of Chester nearby.

Early this summer Wayne's Forts Sandusky, St. Marys, Loramie, Piqua, and Jefferson were dismantled and abandoned, leaving seven others beside those yet held by the British, possession of which he hoped soon to obtain.

The British agents again succeeded in arousing dissatisfaction among some of the Aborigines, and called a council with them for June, 1796, near their Fort Miami. To counteract these influences General Wilkinson invited some of the chiefs to visit him, and, later, he sent Colonel Hamtramck down the Maumee River with a detachment of troops for the purpose of being near those Aborigines who might attend the council. On June 8th and 16th, Hamtramck reported from Camp Deposit at Roche de Bout that:

"I arrived at this place the day before yesterday and have been waiting the result of the Aborigine council at the Miamis fort. It would appear that they are divided in their opinions. White Cap, the principal Shawanese chief, wants to alarm the Aborigines, but I am in hopes that he will not succeed. Blue Jacket is with me, and says he will remain until your arrival. Yesterday some of their chiefs and young men were with me, and assured me of their good intentions toward us. How far this can be depended upon time will determine. . . .

"June 16: . . . Two of my men deserted on the 14th inst. I sent my interpreter and an Aborigine after them. They brought them back last night. I wish they had brought their scalps for I know not what to do with them. Could I have power, at times, to call a general court martial for the trial of deserters, it would save a great deal of time."

Evidently the efforts of the British to regain their lost prestige with the Aborigines by this council did not meet with success.

The United States Special Minister to Great Britain, John Jay, concluded a treaty, November 19, 1794, which was much disliked by many Americans; but which was favorable to the peace of the Northwest Territory, inasmuch as one of its provisions was for the British abandonment of their military posts on American soil on or before the 1st of June, 1796. This treaty was proclaimed as a law by the President, March 1, 1796.

On May 27th General Wilkinson sent Captain Schaumberg, his aide-de-camp, to Detroit, to demand of Colonel England the evacuation of the forts subject to his orders—Fort Lernoult at Detroit, Fort Miami near the foot of the Maumee Rapids, and Fort Michilimackinac; but the Colonel had not received orders to do so from his superior officer, and could not comply with the demand. The British, however, had been building a fort at Malden, near Captain Matthew Elliott's estate, and at the present Amherstburg, on the left bank and near the mouth of the Detroit River or Strait.

The first of June having passed without a movement of the British to vacate the forts, the Secretary of War, with General Wayne as councillor, decided to make one more formal demand for their compliance with the late Jay Treaty. Accordingly Captain Lewis was sent from Philadelphia direct to Lord Dorchester, Governor of Canada. This demand from headquarters was received with civility, and orders were given the Captain, commanding the officers in charge of the forts, east and west, to vacate them to

. . . "such officer belonging to the forces of the United States as shall produce this authority to you for that purpose, who shall precede the troops destined to garrison it by one day, in order that he may have time to view the nature and condition of the works and buildings. . . ."

Upon his return Captain Lewis handed the orders for the eastern forts to Captain Bruff at Albany, New York, and those for the western ones to General Wayne in Philadelphia, who immediately dispatched them to General Wilkinson at Greenville, and he, in turn, sent them to Colonel Hamtramck, who also acted with promptness. Fort Miami was evacuated July 11th, and was at once garrisoned by Captain Marschalk and his command. Fort Lernoult at Detroit was also evacuated the same day, and was immediately occupied by Captain Moses Porter, and, after two days, by Colonel Hamtramck with a considerable garrison.

Thus was possessed, after a further struggle of thirteen years by the young Republic with the loss of much blood, what Great Britain was obligated to at once surrender at the close of the Revolutionary War, according to the Treaty of Paris in 1783.

During the summer of 1796 there was great scarcity of provisions at Detroit for the three hundred American soldiers, as well as for the large number of Aborigines who from habit continued to gather there. Samuel Henley, Acting Quartermaster, went southward to hasten forward supplies by way of the Ohio River to Fort Washington.

He wrote, on August 13th, to General Williams, Quartermaster-General, at Detroit, that:

"The Commissary General gave thirty dollars for the transportation of one barrel of flour from Fort Washington to Fort Wayne.[1] . . . I am well convinced that our public wagonmasters are a poor set of drunken men."

General Wayne, on his return from Philadelphia, arrived at Detroit August 13, 1796, probably by the sloop *Detroit* from Presque Isle, the present Erie, Pennsylvania. He was received with demonstrations of great joy by all persons, including the twelve hundred Aborigines there assembled according to the habit formed by the teachings of the British. He remained at Detroit until November 17th, when he again started for Philadelphia on a small sloop. On this voyage over Lake Erie his system was much irritated and fatigued by the tossings of the storms, and the disease from which he had for some time suffered (understood as gout) made great progress. It could not be allayed after his arrival at Fort Presque Isle, and he there died December 15, 1796,

[1] The form of money most in use here at this time was "York Currency" issued by the Provincial Congress, New York. A few Spanish silver dollars were in circulation, and they were the most valuable of all money seen, being rated at ten shillings each.

aged fifty-one years, eleven months, and fourteen days.[1]

General Wayne served his country well, and with much patriotic fervor. He was a thorough disciplinarian, brave, impetuous, and irresistible in battle; and was successful in inspiring his soldiers at will with these requisites. He was also thoughtful and conservative in planning and equally successful in strategy and assault, as demonstrated on different battle-fields, north and south, during the Revolutionary War. These characteristics were prominent also during his wilderness campaign west of the Allegheny Mountains; and the success and value of this campaign were equalled only by the success and value of his diplomacy in drawing the Savages to Fort Greenville the next year, away from the British, and to the most important of treaties. These last, and greatest, acts of his life should ever be respected as invaluable to his countrymen inasmuch as they settled, favorably to the Union, the first very grave crisis attending the country west of the Allegheny Mountains.

[1] In 1809 his son Colonel Isaac Wayne removed his remains from Presque Isle (Erie, Pennsylvania) to his early home at Radnor, Delaware County, Pennsylvania, where the Society of the Cincinnati of this State erected a modest marble monument to mark his grave.

On the 15th of August, 1796, Winthrop Sargent, Secretary of the Northwestern Territory, proclaimed at Detroit the organization of Wayne County, which included, in addition to the present State of Michigan, the country west of the Cuyahoga River and north of a line extending from Fort Wayne, Indiana, to the south part of Lake Michigan, thence in a northwesterly direction to embrace the Aborigine settlements on the western borders of this lake and its bays.

Thus was brought under the jurisdiction of the United States for the first time this extensive and important country which previously had been (excepting the limited influence of General Wayne's forts) actually under the jurisdiction of County Kent organized in Canada in 1792; but during this time, as previously, it was practically subject to the commandant of the garrison at Detroit, regardless of the Treaty of Paris. The United States Congress contributed to this lamentable condition by its weak efforts for protection; from the trade considerations of some of its members, and, as previously mentioned, from the opinion of many that this invaluable region could not be governed from so great distance from New York or Philadelphia.

The United States, with their western territories, were, however, not yet free from trouble. The Jay Treaty with Great Britain was considered by France as an alteration and suspension of her treaty of 1778 with the United States; and on August 19, 1796, a treaty of alliance, offensive and defensive, was concluded between France and Spain. This at once led to some overt acts by France against the United States on the high seas and to agents of Spain and France again becoming active to alienate these Northwestern and Southwestern Territories from the East. The idea of a Western Confederacy was again advocated by a few persons in Kentucky.

There was again sent northward from the Spanish Governor-General of Louisiana a special emissary in the person of Thomas Power, a versatile Irishman possessing a practical knowledge of the English, French, and Spanish languages, who had previously been in Kentucky and in the Ohio settlements to advance the interests of Spain in the Mississippi Basin. In June, 1797, he again proceeded to Kentucky and addressed influential persons on proposals that were, "in the present uncertain and critical attitude of politics, highly imprudent and dangerous to lay before them on paper," but which were, in effect, that if they would "immediately exert all their influence in impressing on the minds of the inhabitants of the western country a conviction of the necessity of their withdrawing and separating themselves from the Federal Union, and forming an independent government wholly independent of that of the Atlantic States," they would be well rewarded.

"If a hundred thousand dollars distributed in Kentucky would cause it to rise in insurrection, I am certain that the minister, in the present circumstances, would sacrifice them with pleasure; and you may, without exposing yourself too much, promise them to those who enjoy the confidence of the people, with another sum, in case of necessity; and twenty pieces of field artillery."

The Spanish forts in American territory by the Mississippi had not been surrendered to the United States according to the treaty of 1795; and it was reported to the Secretary of State by Winthrop Sargent, Secretary of the Northwest Territory, June 3, 1797, that General Howard, an Irishman commissioned by Spain as Commander-in-Chief, had arrived at St. Louis with upwards of three hundred men, and begun the erection of a formidable fort; that a large party of Aborigines (Delawares) on their way to reinforce the Spaniards had passed down the White River, tributary of the

Wabash, the first week in May bearing a Spanish flag. Further, that the Spanish had, on the Mississippi above the mouth of the Ohio, several galley boats with cannon.

Thomas Power also traversed the Maumee Valley in August, on his way to Detroit to meet General Wilkinson, General Wayne's successor, and other influential men. He was accompanied, or soon followed, by the agents of France, Victor de Collot and M. Warin, who sketched maps of the rivers and country. In a letter from Detroit to Captain Robert Buntin at Vincennes, dated September 4, 1797, Wilkinson mentions having received a letter from the Spanish Governor,

"stating a variety of frivolous reasons for not delivering the [American] posts, and begs that no more troops be sent down the Mississippi. I have put aside all his exceptions, and have called on him in the most solemn manner to fulfill the treaty. . . . Although Mr. Power has brought me this letter it is possible it might be a mask to other purposes; I have therefore, for his accommodation and safety, put him in care of Captain Shaumburgh who will see him safe to New Madrid by the most direct route. I pray you to continue your vigilance, and give me all the information in your power."

France refused to receive the American Minister and permitted many unwise acts of her citizens while the government instigated others. Congress also was now deeply stirred to action, and adopted measures of defence and retaliation; authorizing the formation of a provisional army, about twelve regiments of which were to gather at Fort Washington where boats were to be built to transport them down the Mississippi; commercial intercourse with France was suspended; an act was passed for the punishment of alien and secret enemies of the United States; and for the punishment of treason and sedition. These prompt actions allayed the gathering storm.

The Spaniards of the Mississippi feared an invasion by the British, and President John Adams ordered General Wilkinson on February 4, 1798, to oppose all who should presume to attempt a violation of the laws of the territory of the United States by an expedition through it against their enemies. This implied that the British had designs on the Spanish colony, by way of the Maumee River or the Illinois.

CHAPTER XIII

ADVANCEMENT OF CIVIL GOVERNMENT AND EXTENSION OF THE WEST

Mississippi Territory Organized—General Washington again at the Head of the Federal Army—Spanish Surrender their Forts in United States Territory—First Legislature of Northwestern Territory Convenes—Indiana Territory Organized—Public Lands—Connecticut Cedes her Claims to the United States—Religious Missionaries—Population—Continued British Usurpations—Evidences of the Rising Power of the United States—Treaty with France—Louisiana Territory Purchased—Development of Communication—Military Posts—Ohio Admitted as a State—The Aborigines—Additional Treaties with them—Fort Industry Built—Michigan Territory Organized—Aaron Burr's Last Scheme.

THE Territory of Mississippi was formed by Congress April 7, 1798, and Winthrop Sargent was nominated and approved as its Governor. The vacancy of Secretary of the Northwestern Territory thus made, was filled June 26th by the appointment of William H. Harrison, a competent and rising young man,

Ex-President Washington, July 2, 1798, was chosen Lieutenant-General and Commander-in-Chief of the armies raised and to be raised for the service. There was little to be done, however, that he could not readily delegate to his subordinates.

During this summer, the Spanish vacated their forts on American territory, and, the 5th of October, General Wilkinson took up headquarters at Loftus Heights, where Fort Adams was soon built, on the eastern bank of the Mississippi about six miles north of the 31st degree of north latitude, the then dividing line between the United States and Spanish territory. The prompt action of the United States against intriguers and possible emergencies west of the Alleghenies showed renewed interest in this region, and a spasmodic readiness for its protection, and the danger threatening it was again obviated for a time.

The first Legislature for the Northwestern Territory convened in 1799; and William H. Harrison was chosen the first Delegate, or Representative, of this Territory to the United States Congress.

The difficulties attending the organization and maintenance of government for a vast extent of country, remote from officers and the seat of government, had long been felt, and now became the subject of inquiry by Congress. A committee reported March 3, 1800, that:

"In the three western counties [each then equal in size to a present State] of the Northwest Territory there had been but one court having cognizance of crimes in five years; and the immunity which offenders experience, attracts as to an asylum the most vile and abandoned criminals, and at the same time deters useful and virtuous persons from making settlements in such society."

Thereupon provisions were made for the organization of Indiana Territory. William H. Harrison was appointed its Governor, and the Ordinance of 1787 was to apply for its government.

Four Public Land Offices were established in Ohio Territory, May 10, 1800. The desirability of the United States patent for settlers' lands and more compactness of jurisdiction became more apparent to settlers in Connecticut's Western Reserve. Early in the year 1800, the seekers of homes therein numbered about one thousand, mostly near Lake Erie. On May 30th, the Connecticut Assembly transferred all their claimed rights of jurisdiction to the United States, which action placed all of Ohio Territory upon a uniform land-title basis. This further conduced to the increase in the former Connecticut Reserve of

From 1798-1807

settlements, which now extended westward, and occupied the eastern part of lands of the Aborigines, they receiving payment therefor from the Connecticut Land Company.

Civil organizations ensued; and the second Protestant religious missionary in northern Ohio was sent by the Connecticut Missionary Society to this region during the latter part of the year 1800. He found, however, no township containing more than eleven families.

Near the close of the year 1796, the number of white people within the present limits of Ohio was recorded as about five thousand, mostly settled along the Ohio River and its tributaries within fifty miles. The second United States Census, for the year 1800, showed the population of Ohio Territory, the jurisdiction of which then included what is now eastern Michigan, to be 45,365.

The commandant of the British garrison, after its removal from Detroit to its new Fort Malden, in 1796, continued to ignore the line of United States territory, detachments of soldiers being sent across it at the pleasure of the officials. As late as October 20, 1800, one of the British officers went to Detroit, broke into a private house, and arrested Francis Poquette, using such violence that the victim soon died of the injuries he then received. The British also endeavored to retain their former influence over the American Aborigines.

The rising power of the United States was apparent, however, in the organization, development, and control of this western country. The courage and promptitude more recently exhibited by the government in meeting the many intrigues and aggressions of the Aborigines, the French, Spanish, and of the unduly ambitious Americans, had allayed visionary and chimerical schemes, and given impetus and more stability to the western settlements.

The threatened war with France was happily allayed, and, September 30th, 1800, a treaty with that power was consummated. The ambitions held by Spain for a number of years to possess this region were also defeated, and on October 1st, 1800, she secretly ceded Louisiana back to France after an ownership of thirty-eight years.

Nor did Napoleon's idea of a New France prevail; but rather that wise decision of President Jefferson and Congress for the purchase by the United States, April 30, 1803, of that vast domain styled the Louisiana Purchase. Thus was removed by one master act all objections to

Americans navigating the Mississippi River and trading throughout its course. This purchase also quieted the long-continued agitations, both domestic and foreign, for a western republic, intended by its instigators as an easier means for foreign possession of the country.[1]

Attention was now given to roads, that is the cutting of roadways; to post-offices, and to better means of communication.

In the United States "Estimate of all Posts and Stations where Garrisons will be expedient, and of the Number of Men requisite," made December 3, 1801, but three military posts were mentioned for the territory northwest of the Ohio River, viz.: Michilimackinac, one company of artillery and one of infantry; Detroit, one company of artillery and four of infantry; Fort

[1] Eastern legislators, remnants of the Federalists, who were lukewarm about, or opposed to, protecting the Ohio Country, and at times even in favor of giving it away, were much excited by the suggestion of purchasing Louisiana. Plumer, of New Hampshire, warned the Senate in this wise: "Admit this western world into the Union, and you destroy at once the weight and importance of the eastern States, and compel them to establish a separate independent empire." Griswold, of Connecticut, argued in the House that "The vast unmanageable extent which the accession of Louisiana will give to the United States, the consequent dispersion of our population, and the distribution of the balance which it is so important to maintain between the eastern and western States, threatens, at no very distant day, the subversion of our Union."

Wayne, one company of infantry. In the Act of Congress, March, 1802, for Reduction of the Army, Fort Wayne was styled a "frontier post with garrison of sixty-four men." In the year 1803 this fort had garrison of fifty-one men, viz.: one captain, one surgeon's mate, one first and one second lieutenant, one ensign, four sergeants, four corporals, three musicians, and thirty-five privates.

Since the opinion on March 4, 1802, was that Ohio Territory contained a population of at least sixty thousand people, and the Congressional Committee on this Territory having reported favorably, Congress, April 30th, voted to call a convention of representatives of the Territory meeting November 1st, to frame a Constitution for the proposed State of Ohio. The Constitution was agreed upon and signed with commendable promptness, being completed November 29th; and on February 19, 1803, Ohio was admitted to the Union as a State, the fourth under the general Constitution, and the seventeenth in general number.

After the treaty of Greenville, in 1795, the Aborigines, for a short time, remained reasonably contented with the United States annuity payments to them, and with the amount they received for the peltries obtained by their hunting and trapping. They also received many gratuities from the white settlers among whom they wandered, entering dwellings at will and without ceremony; and they were generally treated with kindly consideration by the white people notwithstanding their want of regard for individual rights in property desired by them. It became more and more apparent, however, that British influence was yet being exerted among them and causing discontent to be fostered among the several tribes, notwithstanding their continued trading of furs to the British, and their spending the money received from the United States freely with them.

Governor Harrison, who was also Superintendent of Aborigine Affairs for Indiana Territory, completed at Fort Wayne, June 7, 1803, the treaty that was begun September 17, 1802, at Vincennes, in which the Eel River, Kaskaskia, Kickapoo, Miami, Piankishaw, Pottawotami, and Wea tribes formally deeded to the United States the lands around Vincennes which had previously been bought of the other tribes; and this act was further confirmed at Vincennes the 7th of August by yet other chiefs. On August 13th the Illinois tribes deeded to the United States a large portion of the country south and east of the Illinois River.

On August 13, 1804, Governor Harrison purchased for the United States the claims of the Delawares to the land between the Wabash and Ohio rivers. He also purchased of the Piankishaws their claims to lands deeded to the United States by the Kaskaskias in 1803. Also by treaty and purchase, the claims of the several tribes to large areas of lands farther west were extinguished.

Fort Industry was built in 1804 on the left bank of the lower Maumee River, at the mouth of Swan Creek, for protection in various ways, and for the convenience of the commissioners who, July 4, 1805, there effected an important treaty with the chiefs and warriors of the Wyandot, Ottawa, Chippewa, Munsee, Delaware, Shawnee, and Pottawotami tribes, and those of the Shawnees and Senecas who lived with the Wyandots at this time, all of whom ceded to the United States their entire claims to the Western Reserve of Connecticut, for, and in consideration of, an annuity of one thousand dollars, in addition to sixteen thousand dollars paid to them by the Connecticut Land Company and the proprietors of the half million acres of Sufferers' Lands (Firelands, lands granted to those who suffered by fire in Connecticut by acts of the British during the Revolutionary War). The small stockade composing Fort Industry was abandoned by the United States soon after this treaty.

Further, a treaty with, and an annuity to, the dissatisfied Pottawotami, Miami, Eel River, and Wea Aborigines near Vincennes, August 21, 1805, induced them to relinquish their claims to the southeastern part of Indiana, which was also bought from the Delawares by the United States on August 18, 1804. These several treaties and purchases, of 1803, '04, '05, including yet another with the Piankishaws on December 30, 1805, extinguished several times over all alleged right of claim to these lands by the Aborigines, not to mention in this connection the purchases and payments of the eighteenth century.

Michigan was organized into a separate Territory by Congress January 11, 1805, the new government to go into effect June 30th. General William Hull was appointed its Governor.

Aaron Burr journeyed, and rejourneyed, through the West and Southwest during the years 1805 and 1806, and rumors became rife of his preparations to invade and conquer Mexico, and to create a western republic of which the country west of the Allegheny Mountains was to form a part. The

Legislature of Ohio ordered, the first part of December, 1806, the seizure of fourteen boats and supplies at Marietta, on the Ohio River, which were about ready to start down the rivers in aid of Burr's scheme. Burr was arrested January 17, 1807, and was released on bail, which he forfeited. He was again arrested while endeavoring to escape, was subjected to trial at Richmond, Virginia, and was acquitted. Thus failed the fourth and weakest effort to wrest this western region from the United States.

During these years of scheming by restless, designing persons, and of apprehension by the government, there was considerable strengthening by the United States of the garrisons of Forts Washington, Wayne, and Detroit; and preparations were made for their active service. The increasing aggressions of the British, and the conduct of Aaron Burr, were reasons for this military activity.

CHAPTER XIV

CONSPIRACY OF THE BRITISH, TECUMSEH, AND THE PROPHET

Further Treaties with, and Payments to, the Aborigines—The British Continue Meddlesome—Reservations—United States Settlers by the Lower Maumee River—Land for Highways Treated for—Illinois Territory Organized—Another British-Savage Trouble Gathering—Trading Posts for the Aborigines Established—Reports of Gathering Trouble from United States Military Posts—The British Continue to Trade Intoxicating Liquors to American Aborigines in Opposition to Law.

ON January 27, 1807, Henry Dearborn, Secretary of War, sent a commission to William Hull, Governor of Michigan Territory, and Superintendent of Aborigine Affairs there, with instructions to hold a treaty council with the Aborigines, who were becoming very restless and aggressive. Governor Hull issued a call to the different tribes for a council at Detroit; but the Aborigines did not attend. Two other calls were sent to them, and President Jefferson directed him to communicate to them the continued friendly intentions and offices of the United States. The sequel proved that their desires to respond to the invitations to council had been thwarted by Captain Alexander McKee, the British agent. Finally, they evaded McKee and his aids, and went to Detroit for council, in which they proclaimed the intrigue of the British to again more closely ally them to their aid "for the war likely to ensue with the United States."

Between seven and eight hundred Aborigines had been invited to Malden, now Amherstburg, where intoxicating beverages and promises prevailed. During October and November many hundreds of these Aborigines were unavoidably fed at Detroit by Governor Hull, while on their way to and from the British Fort Malden influence, and also during the council, notwithstanding the direction of the Secretary of War, that from fifty to one hundred was as great a number as ought to be allowed to attend.

A prominent feature of this council with Governor Hull, and one that was remembered and repeated by the Aborigines, was the expression of President Jefferson that the Aborigines should remain quiet spectators and not participate in the quarrels of others, particularly those of the white people; and that the United States was strong enough to fight its own battles; and that it was evidence of weakness on the part of any people to want the aid of the Aborigines.

Finally, at Detroit, November 17, 1807, a treaty was effected with the Chippewa, Ottawa, Pottawotami, and Wyandot tribes in which they deeded to the United States all their claims to the country north of the middle of the Maumee River, from its mouth in Maumee Bay and Lake Erie, to the mouth of the Auglaize River; thence extending north to the latitude of the south part of Lake Huron, thence east to and southward along the Canadian boundary. For their claim to this territory, as in all former treaties and transfers, they were well paid, receiving ten thousand dollars in money and goods as first payment, and were to receive an annuity of two thousand and four hundred dollars. They were given, also, the option of money, goods, implements of husbandry, and domestic animals, from which to choose. Of these sums the Chippewas received one third, the Ottawas one third, and the Pottawotamis and Wyandots each one sixth. This treaty further informed them that

"the United States, to manifest their liberality, and disposition to encourage the said Aborigines in agriculture, further stipulate to furnish the said Aborigines with two blacksmiths during the term of ten years, one to reside with the Chippewas at Saginaw, and the other to reside with the Ottawas at the Maumee [presumably at the mouth of the Auglaize]. Said blacksmiths are to do such work for the said nations as shall be most useful to them."

The principal object of this treaty and purchase was to keep the Aborigines as far from the British as possible. As in former treaties, however, the Aborigines were to have the privilege of hunting for game animals on the ceded lands as long as the lands remained the distinctive property of the United States, and during the good behavior of the Aborigines.

Certain tracts of this land were also reserved for the exclusive use of certain prominent Aborigines, viz.: Six miles square on the north bank of the Maumee above Roche de Bout "to include the village where Tondagame [Tontogany], or the dog, now lives" (probably near the present Grand Rapids, Ohio). Another reservation for them was

"three miles square above the twelve miles square ceded to the United States at the Treaty of Greenville, including what is called Presque Isle [on left bank of Maumee River below the present Waterville]; also four miles square on the Miami [Maumee] Bay, including the villages where Meshkemau and Waugau now live. . . . It is further understood and agreed, that whenever the reservations cannot conveniently be laid out in squares, they shall be laid out in parallelograms or other figures as found most practicable and convenient, so as to obtain the area specified in miles; and in all cases they are to be located in such manner and in such situations as not to interfere with any improvements of the French or other white people, or any former cession."

American settlers continued to gather in Ohio, and some took residence on these United States Reservations at the Foot of the Rapids of the Maumee. The necessity for roads to connect the settlements in Ohio with those in Michigan becoming more apparent, Governor Hull was directed to secure cession of lands for such roads from the Aborigines. Accordingly, at Brownstown, Michigan, November 25, 1808, a treaty was held with the sachems, chiefs, and warriors of the Chippewa, Ottawa, Pottawotami, Shawnee, and Wyandot tribes, in which they quit-claimed a tract of land, one hundred and twenty feet in width, for a road from the foot of the lowest rapids of the Maumee River eastward to the western line of the Connecticut Reserve; also all the land within one mile of each side of this roadway for the settlement of white people:

"Also a tract of land for road only, of one hundred and twenty feet in width to run southwardly from what is called Lower Sandusky [now Fremont, Ohio] to the boundary line established by the Treaty of Greenville; with the privilege of taking, at all times, such timber and other materials from the adjacent lands as may be necessary for making and keeping in repair the said road, with the bridges that may be required along the same."

No compensation was given the Aborigines in money or merchandise for these roadways, as "they were desirable and beneficial to the Aborigine nations as well as to the United States," reads a clause in the deed of quit-claim.

Indiana Territory, from its organization in 1802, had extended to the Mississippi River. The settlements had increased to such numbers, however, that the "Illinois Country" was organized into Illinois Territory, February 3, 1809.

For several years, the Aborigines had manifested an increasing restlessness, which was attributed by Captain Dunham and other American officers to the influence of the British who were trading among them, and those at Fort Malden where they received supplies.

The idea first taught to the Savages by the early French, in opposition to the British, first exploited by Pontiac in 1763 against the British, and then amplified with greater force by the British among the Savages against the Americans from the beginning of the Revolutionary War— of a confederation of all the tribes, and that all lands should be claimed by them collectively, and that no claims should be disposed of, nor any advance of the Americans upon the lands be permitted—was being revived, and again urged before the Aborigines by the British and a few Frenchmen in their interest. In 1805 Tecumseh, an energetic Shawnee brave, began therefrom to repeat the history of Pontiac, the Americans being the people conspired against.

The increasing purchases of claims by the United States were for the purpose of getting the Aborigines farther from British influence, and getting American settlers between them and the British. The object of getting the Aborigines on small tracts of land was that they might be led away from their roaming, hunting habits, and thereby be easier led to agricultural pursuits, and into closer sympathy with Americans; but these worthy objects and acts in their interests were reacting against the Americans.

With the rapid increase of settlers on the lands purchased, and their beginning to clear away the forest; the organization of territories, states, and counties, with their courts and closer government, came the exciting of apprehension among the lawless traders, agents, and loungers in the camps of the Aborigines, the chronically meddlesome British, from trade interests at least, inciting them to renewed intrigues.

Tecumseh's reputed brother Elskwatawa had recently removed with other Shawnees from the Scioto River, Ohio, to the Tippecanoe River, Indiana, where he soon gained something of a notoriety as a sorcerer. He began to tell of his dreams and visions, and to claim the knowledge and power of a prophet inspired and commissioned by the Great Spirit to lead the Aborigines back to the condition of their ancestors before the coming of the Americans. All of this chicanery forcibly appealed to the younger Aborigines and warriors, who were ever ready to embrace any superstition or act offering exploitation. The remarkable pretensions of Elskwatawa spread from the Shawnee town by the Tippecanoe River to other and distant tribes, being carried by runners, including Tecumseh, who travelled rapidly from tribe to tribe between Lake Erie and the Mississippi River, and from the upper lakes to the Gulf of Mexico.

These actions of Tecumseh, the "Prophet,"

and many of the younger Aborigines who were anxious for any new movement promising excitement, were understood by Governor Harrison as a concerted effort to marshal the Aborigines as British allies again against the United States.

Since the campaign of General Wayne a new generation of young Aborigines, fed from the rations supplied to their parents by the United States, had developed into warriors anxious for excitement and ready at short notice to follow any leader whose project appeared probable to gratify their savage impulses.

Letters were soon received by the Secretary of War, from the several military posts throughout the western country, regarding the increasing hostility of the Aborigines, and their threatenings to exterminate Americans, also of their being aided by the British.

General William Clark wrote from St. Louis, April 5, 1809, that the "Prophet's emissaries" had been industriously employed, during the latter part of the winter and spring, privately councilling with, and attempting to seduce to war against the frontier settlements, the Kickapoos, Saukeys, and other bands by the Mississippi and Illinois rivers.

Captain William Wells wrote from Fort Wayne,

the 8th of April, that the Aborigines appeared to be agitated respecting the conduct, and as they said the intentions, of the Shawnee Prophet.

"The Chippewas, Ottawas, and Pottawotamis are hurrying away from him, and say that their reason for so doing is because he has told them to receive the tomahawk from him and destroy all the white people at Vincennes and Ohio, as low down as the mouth of the Ohio and as high up as Cincinnati; that the Great Spirit had directed that they should do so, at the same time threatening them with destruction if they refused to comply with what he proposed."

General Clark wrote from St. Louis, April 30th:

"I have the honor to enclose you a copy of a letter which confirms my suspicions of the British interference with our Indian affairs in this country. The following is an extract from the letter from Boilvin: ' . . . I am at present in the fire receiving Aborigine news every day. A chief of the Puant nation appears to be employed by the British to get all the nations of Aborigines to Malden to see their fathers the British, who tell them that they pity them in their situation with the Americans, because the Americans had taken their lands and their game; that they must join and send them off from their lands. They said they had but one father that had helped them in their misfortunes, and that they should assemble, defend their father, and keep their lands.' It appears that four English subjects have been at Riviere a la Roche this winter in disguise; they have been there to get the nations together and send them on the American frontiers."

Governor Harrison wrote from Vincennes, May 3, 1809, of his "decided opinion that the Prophet will attack our settlements. About eight days ago he had with him about three hundred and fifty warriors well armed with rifles; they have also bows and arrows, war clubs, and a kind of spear."

The Factor (Agent) of the American Trading Post at Sandusky, S. Tupper, wrote, June 7th, that, "the conduct of the British traders in introducing spirituous liquors among the Aborigines in this part of the country, and their determined hostility to the measures of our Government, have long been subjects of complaint; and their infamous stories have embarrassed our operations."

Governor Hull wrote from Detroit, June 16th, that, "the influence of the Prophet has been great, and his advice to the Aborigines injurious to them and to the United States. We have the fullest evidence that his object has been to form a combination of them in hostility to the United States. The powerful influence of the British has been exerted in a way alluring to the savage character."

Complaints also came to the Secretary of War that British agents were inciting the Aborigines along the western shore of Lake Michigan, and supplying them with guns and ammunition.

General Harrison wrote from Vincennes, July 5th, that

"The Shawnee Prophet and about forty followers arrived here about a week ago. He denies most strenuously any participation in the late combination to attack our settlements. . . . I must confess that my suspicions of his guilt have been rather strengthened than diminished at each interview I have had with him since his arrival. He acknowledged that he received an invitation to war against us from the British last fall, and that he was apprised of the intention of the Sacs, Foxes, etc., early in the spring, and was warmly solicited to join in their league. . . . The result of all my enquiries on the subject is, that the late combination was produced by British intrigue and influence in anticipation of war between them and the United States. It was, however, premature and ill-judged."

Governor Harrison, in council with Aborigines at Fort Wayne, September 30, 1809, succeeded, however, in further purchasing their claims to two tracts of land in Indiana Territory west of the Greenville treaty line and adjoining former purchases, the stipulated price being permanent annuities of five hundred dollars to the Delawares, five hundred dollars to the Miamis, two hundred and fifty dollars to the Eel River Miamis, and five hundred to the Pottawotamis. The Miamis, by separate article of same date, as additional compensation, were promised that at Fort Wayne the next spring, they would receive domestic animals to the value of five hundred dollars, and a like number for the two following years; and that an armorer should be also maintained at Fort Wayne for the use of the Aborigines as heretofore. In treaty with the Kickapoos at Vincennes, December 9th, Governor Harrison purchased claims to land northwest of the Wabash River, adjoining the Vincennes tract, the consideration being a permanent annuity of four hundred dollars, and goods to the amount of eight hundred dollars. By this last treaty the Miamis were to receive a further annuity of two hundred dollars, and the Eel River tribes or bands one hundred dollars each.

CHAPTER XV

RESULTS OF FURTHER REMISSNESS OF THE GOVERNMENT

Regarding Trading Posts or Agencies—Conspiracy of the British and Tecumseh Deepens—Reports from Military Posts—Battle of Tippecanoe—Continued Organization and Depredations by the Allied Enemies of the United States—Missouri Territory Organized—More Cannibalism by the Savages.

TRADING Agencies had been established among the Aborigine tribes several years after, and according to, the suggestions of General Wayne, after the treaty of Greenville in 1795. The report to the Secretary of War, December 31, 1809, of J. Mason, Superintendent of these Agencies, styled Factories, possesses features of interest in this connection. There were at this date twelve establishments of this character, eight of which were in the South and Southwest, viz.: Fort Hawkins, Georgia; Chickasaw Bluffs, Mississippi Territory; Fort St. Stephens by the

Mobile River; Fort Osage by the Missouri River; Fort Madison by the upper Mississippi River; Natchitoches by the Red River of the South; Fort Wayne at the head of the Maumee River; Chicago at the southwestern part of Lake Michigan, established in 1805; Sandusky, Ohio, established in 1806; Detroit, established in 1802, and discontinued in 1805 on account of its nearness to the British supply house at Fort Malden; and the Agency at Michilimackinac, established in 1808.

The net assets of these Agencies or Factories at the close of the year 1809 was $235,461.64. The amount of appropriations at the close of 1811 was $300,000 exclusive of officers' salaries, which then amounted to about $35,000 annually. From 1807 to 1811 inclusive, the profit was $14,171. The southern Factories reported losses, principally on account of the greater difficulty of communication.

Details of but one of these Factories will be given. The principal one, at Fort Wayne, was organized in 1802. Colonel John Johnston was the Factor in 1809, with salary of $1000 per year, and subsistence allowance of $365. William Oliver, his clerk, received salary of $250 a year and $150 for subsistence. The inventory of October 5th showed: Merchandise, Peltries, etc., on hand, $5,020.75; Accounts Receivable, per return of March, $2,112.72; Buildings, estimated at about one half of cost, $500. Merchandise forwarded by the government to Fort Wayne, July 28th, and not included in the above amounted to $4,686.87.

The peltries taken in exchange for merchandise at these Trading Houses were: beaver, first quality, two dollars each, second quality, one dollar; dressed deer skins, one dollar and fifty cents; wolf skins, one dollar; muskrat, raccoon, wildcat, and fox skins, twenty-five cents each; otter, two dollars and fifty cents; bear, first quality, one dollar and fifty cents, second quality, one dollar. Tallow, twelve and a half cents a pound, and beeswax at twenty cents also entered into the accounts.

The British continued, however, to command most of the beaver and other of the best fur trade.

Tecumseh and the Prophet continued active. The additional councils and purchases of claims to land at Fort Wayne and Vincennes were alleged as new incentives. General Harrison wrote to the Secretary of War, June 14, 1810, that:

"I have received information from various sources which has produced entire conviction in my mind, that the Prophet is organizing a most extensive combination against the United States." Another letter, dated the 26th of June, informs that: "Winemac [a friendly Aborigine] assured me that the Prophet not long since proposed to the young men to murder the principal chiefs of all the tribes; observing that their hands would never be untied until this was effected; that these were the men who had sold their lands, and who would prevent opposing the encroachments of the white people. An Iowa Indian informs me that two years ago this summer an agent from the British arrived at the Prophet's town and, in his presence, delivered a message with which he was charged, the substance of which was to urge the Prophet to unite as many tribes as he could against the United States, but not to commence hostilities until they gave the signal."[1]

On July 11, 1810, General Harrison again wrote that:

"I have received a letter from Fort Wayne which confirms the information of the hostile designs and combination of the Indians. The people in the

[1] The reader will bear in mind in this connection the strained relations of the United States and Great Britain which had existed since the Revolutionary War, and which frequently received fresh incentives from the impressment of American seamen, the searchings of American ships, the unjust discriminations in trade, as well as overt acts in this western country. The continued arrogance and aggressiveness of the British in Canada, with their efforts to control the Savages throughout the United States, show that the British ulterior designs on this western country remained unabated.

neighborhood where the horses were stolen are so much alarmed that they are collecting together for their defense."

Again on July 18th:

"From the Iowas I learn that the Sacs and Foxes have actually received the tomahawk and are ready to strike whenever the Prophet gives the signal. A considerable number of Sacs went some time since to see the British Superintendent and, on the first instant, fifty more passed Chicago for the same destination. A Miami chief who has just returned from his annual visit to Malden, after having received the accustomed donation of goods was thus addressed by the British agent: 'My son keep your eyes fixed on me; my tomahawk is now up; be you ready, but do not strike until I give the signal.'"

General Clark wrote from St. Louis, July 20th, that:

"A few weeks ago the post-rider on his way from Vincennes to this place was killed, and the mail lost; since that time we have had no communication with Vincennes. A part of the Sacs and the greatest part of the Kickapoos who reside east of the Mississippi have been absent some time on a visit to the Indian Prophet. One hundred and fifty Sacs are on a visit to the British Agent by invitation, and a smaller party on a visit to the Island of St. Joseph in Lake Huron."

On July 25th, General Harrison again wrote in part as follows:

"There can be no doubt of the designs of the Prophet and the British Agent of Indian Affairs [Alexander McKee?] to do us injury. This agent is a refugee from the neighborhood of———[Pittsburg] and his implacable hatred of his native country prompted him to take part with the Aborigines in the battle between them and General Wayne's army. [See *ante*.] He has, ever since his appointment to the principal agency, used his utmost endeavors to excite hostilities, and the lavish manner in which he is allowed to scatter presents amongst them, shews that his government participates in his enmity and authorizes his measures."

Governor Hull wrote from Detroit, July 27th, in part as follows:

"Large bodies of Indians from the westward and southward continue to visit the British post at Amherstburg [Malden] and are supplied with provisions, arms, ammunition, etc. Much more attention is paid to them than usual."

On August 7th, Captain John Johnston, Agent of the Fort Wayne Trading Post, wrote:

"Since writing you on the 25th ultimo, about one hundred Sawkeys [Sacs] have returned from the British Agent who supplied them liberally with everything they stood in want of. The party received forty-seven rifles and a number of fusils [flintlock muskets] with plenty of powder and lead. This is sending firebrands into the Mississippi country inasmuch as it will draw numbers of our Aborigines to the British side in the hope of being treated with the same liberality."

On August 1, 1810, General Harrison reported that a number of the inhabitants of the northern frontier of the Jeffersonville district had been driven away by the Aborigines, and much of their property destroyed.

The Secretary of War received many other letters from the widely separated posts, evidencing the continued preparations of the Savages for war, under the incitements of the British. But few additional excerpts will be here given. February 6, 1811, Captain Johnston reported from Fort Wayne:

"—— has been at this place. The information derived from him is the same I have been in possession of for several years, to wit: the intrigues of the British agents and partisans in creating an influence hostile to our people and government, within our territory. I do not know whether a garrison [fort] is to be erected on the Wabash or not; but every consideration of sound policy urges the early establishment of a post somewhere contiguous to the Prophet's residence."

It is well to bear in mind in this connection the continued echoes of the remnant of the Federalists of New England, who yet desired to ignore the western country, and who had done much toward the ignoring of the aggressions of the British in the Ohio Country, and, finally, opposed the War of 1812 to correct these abuses. January 14, 1811, Josiah Quincy, Representative from Massachusetts, spoke in the House in part as follows:

"I am compelled to declare it as my deliberate opinion that, if this bill [for the admission of Orleans (Louisiana) as a State] passes, the bonds of this Union are virtually dissolved; that the States which compose it are free from their moral obligations; and that as it will be the right of all, so it will be the duty of some, to prepare definitely for a separation amicably, if they can, violently, if they must."

Hostilities were continued to the westward, some murders and captivities of Americans being reported; and some blockhouses were built along the frontier for the refuge and defence of the remaining settlers.

Governor Harrison had not remained idle. He had instituted preparations for defence, and for advance movements. By appointment he was visited by the chief leader of the hostile Aborigines, his written report of the visit, August 6, 1811, being in part as follows:

"The Shawnee Chief Tecumseh has made a visit to this place with about three hundred Indians, though he promised to bring but a few attendants; *his intentions hostile*, though he found us prepared for him. Tecumseh did not set out until yesterday; he then descended the Wabash attended by twenty men on his way to the southward. After having visited the Creeks and Choctaws he is to visit the Osages, and return by the Missouri. The spies say his object in coming with so many was to demand a retrocession of the late purchase [of Aborigine claims to land]. At the moment he was promising to bring but a few men with him he was sending in every direction to collect his people. That he meditated a blow at this time was believed by almost all the neutral Aborigines."

Governor Harrison reported, September 11th, from Vincennes as follows:

"——— states that almost every Indian from the country above this had been or was gone to Malden on a visit to the British Agent. We shall probably gain our destined point at the moment of their return. If then the British agents are really endeavoring to instigate the Aborigines to make war upon us, we shall be in their neighborhood at the very moment when the impressions which have been made against us are most active in the minds of the savages. ——— succeeded in getting the chiefs together at Fort Wayne, though he found them all preparing to go to Malden. The result of the council discovered that the whole tribes (including the Weas and Eel Rivers, for they are all Miamis) were about equally divided in favor of the Prophet and the United States.

—— reports that all the Aborigines of the Wabash have been or now are on a visit to the British Agent at Malden; he has never known more than one-fourth as many goods given to the Aborigines as they are now distributing. He examined the share of one (not a chief) and found that he had received an elegant rifle, twenty-five pounds of powder, fifty pounds of lead, three blankets, three strouds of cloth, ten shirts, and several other articles. He says every Aborigine is furnished with a gun (either rifle or fusil) and an abundance of ammunition. A trader of this country was lately in the King's store at Malden, and was told that the quantity of goods for the Indian Department which had been sent out this year, exceeded that of common years by £20,000 sterling. It is impossible to ascribe this profusion to any other motive than that of instigating the Aborigines to take up the tomahawk; it cannot be to secure their trade for all the peltries collected on the waters of the Wabash in one year if sold on the London market would not pay the freight of the goods which have been given to the Aborigines."

Tecumseh and the Prophet had been advising discontinuance of trade with Americans. Action on this advice led to some clandestine trading, to more fraudulent practices by the Aborigines, and to their violence. But the principal result was observed as an additional incentive to turn the Savages to the British whose lavish gifts had already drawn nearly all of them to Fort Malden.

Meetings of citizens along the frontier were

held during the summer of 1811; and memorials stating the depredations and murders by the Aborigines, accompanied by petitions for protection, were sent by them to President Madison.

Governor Harrison was given additional regular troops and militia, and the second week in October they advanced up the Wabash towards the Prophet's town by the Tippecanoe River to stop his influence for further murderous raids. Peace messengers were sent forward, but they were violently treated, and on the night of the 10th a sentinel of the American command was severely wounded by the Prophet's adherents. Governor Harrison commanded the Americans in person. He advanced cautiously and, on the 6th of November, meeting some of the Prophet's messengers near his town, made an agreement for a council the next morning. But, true to the treacherous nature of the Savages, they made a stealthy attack in the dark about a quarter past four o'clock in the morning, when, in the words of Governor Harrison's report, "they manifested a ferocity uncommon to them. To their savage fury our troops, nineteen twentieths of whom had not before been in battle, opposed that cool and deliberate valor which is characteristic of the Christian soldier." The Savages retreated.

The Americans in this Battle of Tippecanoe numbered a few over seven hundred; and the number of Savages was estimated as nearly the same. The American loss was sixty-two killed and one hundred and twenty-six wounded. The loss of the Savages was estimated at a larger number.

The condition of the frontier settlements was but little, if any, improved by this defeat of the Shawnee Prophet's army. To dishearten the Savages seriously, it was necessary to give them a crushing defeat, or a series of defeats. Depredations and murders continued in the West, and grave apprehensions pervaded the entire country.

Among the petitioners to the President and Congress for protection, were the prominent citizens of the Territory of Michigan, living at Detroit, who gave statistics from which the following are extracted, viz.: The population of the Territory, December 10, 1811, was given as four thousand seven hundred and sixty-two, about four fifths of whom were French, the remainder being largely Americans, with a few British, and some servants of African blood.[1]

---

[1] African slaves were brought into this western region by the Aborigines, and were taken to Detroit from an early date. They were bought first by the French, and later by the British, army officers, and merchants, by whom they were retained as servants for many years.

They were distributed in nine principal settlements each settlement having a "double frontier" —the British on one side, the Savages on the other. The first three of these settlements were named as: 1, the mouth of the Maumee River; 2, the River Raisin; 3, the River Huron, in Michigan Territory. The other settlements were at Detroit, and northward, and westward. There were two forts, Detroit with a garrison of ninety-four soldiers, and Michilimackinac with seventy-nine soldiers. Additional forts were petitioned for, with stronger garrisons, and cavalry.

Wandering bands of hostile Aborigines and "British emissaries" continued to visit every camp, and Fort Malden. Had the petitions of the settlers for more forts and cavalry been granted, and these hostile mischief-makers been arrested and imprisoned, the influence of the "Prophet" and of the British could have been greatly reduced and many American lives saved. The policy of forbearance, delay, and hoping for peace was continued until long after the British and their savage allies were again thoroughly organized.

Governor Howard of Missouri Territory wrote March 19, 1812, detailing depredations and "most barbarous murders" by Savages; and the letters of like import from Captain Nathan Heald were frequent from Chicago, including the report of killing and eating two Americans by Winnebagoes at the lead mines near the Mississippi River.

The Trading Agent at Fort Wayne, then Major Benjamin F. Stickney, after reporting a grand council of twelve tribes by the Wabash River, wrote May 25th, what he had before written to Governor Hull, viz.:

"The time appears to have arrived when it is necessary, if possible, to cut off all communication between the Indians within the territory of the United States, and Canada."

This was a very tardy suggestion of a policy the enforcement of which should have seemed a necessity many years before this date. Tribe after tribe and band after band of the Aborigines, including several hundred Ottawas of the lower Maumee, had been enticed to remove to the Tippecanoe, or to near Malden, and again to ally themselves closely with the British for a general war.

CHAPTER XVI

SAD BEGINNING OF THE WAR FOR INDEPENDENCE

Tardy Action of Congress—Declaration of War against Great Britain—This War of 1812 the Real War for Independence—The Army of the Northwest the First in the Field—Forts McArthur, Necessity, Findlay, and Miami Built—Sad Inefficiency of General Hull—He Orders the Abandonment of Fort Dearborn—Massacre and Cannibalism by British Allies—Hull Surrenders Fort at Detroit without Effort for Defence—Brave and Patriotic Work by Captain Brush.

NOTWITHSTANDING the numerous reports of many American agents and officers, during several years of depredations and murderings by the Savages, and the accumulated evidence of their incitement by British traders, other agents, and officers, it was not until June 13, 1812, that the committee of Congress reported it proved that the British had been working among these Aborigines with the intention of securing them as allies against the United States;

that the British had incited them to hostilities and presented them with weapons of warfare which had already been used against the Americans; and that it was the duty of the President of the United States to use the necessary means to protect the frontiers from the attacks with which they were yet threatened.

The war cloud that had been lowering for several years, settled into a formal declaration of war against Great Britain, June 18, 1812, on account of the enemy's interference with American trade, enforced by a blockade; the search of American vessels; the impressment of American seamen, and the encouragement of the Aborigines in their savagery against Americans. This last charge was yet far more apparent in the West than to the general public in the East and was, as yet, scarcely mentioned by those highest in authority in the East.

This was to be the real war for independence from Great Britain, as foreseen by Benjamin Franklin; the war of 1775-1783 was only Revolutionary.

Governor William Hull, of Michigan Territory, was in Washington during part of the winter and spring of 1812, and he urged the President to increase the military force in the Northwest; and for the third time he called attention to the positive necessity for an American naval fleet on Lake Erie.

The President made requisition early in April upon Governor Return J. Meigs of Ohio for twelve hundred militia to be ready for immediate march to Detroit. He also appointed Commander Stewart, Agent on Lake Erie, and ordered the building of vessels for defence.

On April 8th, Governor Hull was commissioned Brigadier-General in the United States army, and he was ordered to take charge of the Ohio troops. It appears that this was against his desire, and it was surely a very serious mistake. Hull arrived May 25th at Dayton, Ohio, the place of rendezvous, and the volunteer troops were at once given to his command by Governor Meigs. They moved northward June 1st to Urbana, where they were joined by the Fourth Regiment of United States troops, which the President had ordered forward from Vincennes.

It was the desire of General Hull to go as direct to Detroit as practicable, and this course led through a trackless forest until arrival at the Maumee River a little below Roche de Bout. Colonel Duncan McArthur's First Regiment was detached to cut a road from Urbana, which was done to the Scioto River near the present Kenton, and there they built two blockhouses and connected them with stockades, which, later, received the name Fort McArthur.

The army arrived at this post June 19th. The Second Regiment, under Colonel James Findlay, was here detached to cut and bridge a road onward. On June 22d, Fort McArthur was garrisoned by Captain Dill's company, and leaving the sick in his care, the army moved forward. Heavy rains made the way across the morasses at the headwaters of the Blanchard River well-nigh impassable, and, after a laborious struggle, and under great annoyance from the small flies and mosquitoes, they were obliged to halt sixteen miles from Fort McArthur. Here were built another stockade and houses which were named Fort Necessity. With lessening food supplies, the horses and oxen were put on short allowance, and rearrangements were made whereby the wagons were to be relieved of more of their burden by packs on the horses "and every man who could make a packsaddle was detailed on that business; but as soon as a sufficient number of saddles were made the order was rescinded, and the saddles were deposited in the blockhouses."

The weather improving, the army advanced and, after three days, arrived at the Blanchard River, on the left bank of which Colonel Findlay's detachment had nearly completed a stockaded enclosure about one hundred and fifty feet square, with a blockhouse at each corner, and a ditch in front. General Hull gave this place of refuge in the forest the name Fort Findlay. It was situated but a few squares north of the present court-house in the city of Findlay, Ohio.

A messenger, Colonel Dunlap, here delivered to General Hull, on June 24th, an order from the Secretary of War for the army to proceed at once to Detroit and there expect further orders. This order was dated the morning of June 18th, the day that war was declared, but no mention of this act was made in the order. Colonel McArthur, however, received communication the same day from Chillicothe, stating on authority of Thomas Worthington, then United States Senator from Ohio, that war would be proclaimed before this writing could be delivered to him. This letter was shown to General Hull who, from his previous information, knew that war was imminent.

President Madison and William Eustis, Secretary of War, early provided for three armies for the prosecution of the War of 1812, viz.: The Army of the Northwest, under General Hull, which was the first in the field; the Army of the Center, under Solomon Van Rensselaer, whose headquarters were at Niagara; and the Army of the North, under General Joseph Bloomfield, whose head-quarters were at Plattsburg, New York.

The object of the remaining part of this book is to follow the movements, failures, and successes of the Army of the Northwest, which will be credited with turning the contest against the British, and with the saving of the region west of the Allegheny Mountains, for the second time, at least, to the United States.

General Hull directed Colonel Lewis Cass, with the Third Regiment, to cut and prepare a road northward from Fort Findlay. Much of the heavy baggage was stored at this fort, to be forwarded as desired, and the army proceeded as soon as practicable. After a few days' march, they arrived at the Maumee River, opposite the site of General Wayne's battle-field of Fallen Timber, where encampment was made for the night. Fording the river at the rapids here, the next encampment was made near a small village of American settlers, and at the site of the British Fort Miami of 1794-1796.

Here the schooner *Cuyahoga* under Captain Chapin was chartered for Detroit, and loaded with much of the heavier baggage, including entrenching implements, hospital stores, the heaviest part of the officers' personal effects, and even thoughtlessly including the General's commission, the instructions from the Secretary of War, and the complete muster rolls of the army. Thirty soldiers were detailed as guard for the schooner, which also carried as passengers the wives of three subordinate officers.

The sequel proved that it would have been far better for the American cause had General Hull also gone with his private papers, direct to the British. Captain McPherson, of Cincinnati, here suggested to the General that war must have been declared, and that the schooner would be captured by the enemy. The *Cuyahoga*, accompanied by a sloop carrying the sick under care of Surgeon's Mate James Reynolds, sailed, however, from the Maumee River, July 1, 1812, the former to be captured by the British next day, when passing Fort Malden. The sloop was belated and, going up the shallower channel west of Bois Blanc Island, evaded the enemy and arrived at Detroit July 3d.

Lieutenant Davidson and twenty-five privates

were detached to build and occupy a blockhouse at the ruins of Fort Miami,[1] and, July 1st, the army continued the march northward through the best cleared country in the West, it having been the highway, with many settlements, of the French and British, for one hundred and fifty years or more.

General Hull did not formally learn of the declaration of war until the afternoon of July 2d, when he was overtaken near Frenchtown (the present Monroe, Michigan) by a messenger with such information from the Secretary of War; and he here also learned of the capture of his schooner. The British garrison at Fort Malden had previously received notification of the war, and was alert for action. Fort Michilimackinac (later Mackinac, and Mackinaw) with a garrison of fifty-seven soldiers was surrendered to a far superior force of British and Savages July 17th, the commandant, Lieutenant Porter Hicks, first learning at their demand for surrender that war was declared.

Late in July, Hull ordered the abandonment of Fort Dearborn, Chicago, Captain William Wells

---

[1] *See* the article on the six Forts Miami in the *Ohio Archæological and Historical Quarterly*, April, 1903, vol. xii., p. 120 *et seq.*, by Charles E. Slocum.

bearing the order from Fort Wayne. Members of the garrison, and others, including Captain Wells, who had been a very efficient scout, interpreter, and soldier with Wayne, and later, suffered massacre on leaving the fort, by Savages who ate the heart and part of the body of Wells particularly.

Governor Meigs, Thomas Worthington, and Jeremiah Morrow, as United States Commissioners, held a council at Piqua, Ohio, August 15th, with such representatives of the Aborigines as could be gathered, for the purpose of securing their neutrality with the British. A number of the Ohio tribes were represented, but little could be done with them, they having heard the report from Michilimackinac and Chicago.

Full account of the weak conduct of General Hull, which has been several times and fully written, will not be given space here. It culminated, August 16th, in the surrender to the British of Detroit, with nearly two thousand American soldiers, without any effort toward resistance having been made. This surrender was an irreparable loss to the Northwestern Army, and of corresponding value to the enemy. As heretofore seen on these pages, this post had for many years been a great vantage ground for the

British; and the surrender also carried to the enemy two thousand and four hundred stand of arms, besides those in the arsenal; also of cannon: iron, nine 24-pounders, five 9-, three 6-, four 2-, and two 1-pounders; and of howitzers, one 8-inch and one 5½-inch; these according to the British official returns.

The Ohio volunteers in this unfortunate army were paroled, and sent across Lake Erie to Cleveland, whence they walked to their respective homes. They were exchanged in March or early April, 1813. General Hull and the United States troops were retained as prisoners of war, and were sent to Montreal.

An additional two hundred and thirty volunteers, under Captain Henry Brush, with one hundred beef cattle and other food supplies, sent by Governor Meigs to reinforce the army at Detroit, were held by the British from advancing beyond the river Raisin from the first days of August, without relief from Detroit. Hull included this force in his surrender; but when Captain Elliott, son of the notorious Captain Matthew Elliott, and his attendants came to claim this prize, Captain Brush placed them under arrest and immediately started his command and supplies southward, and conducted them back to Governor Meigs.

CHAPTER XVII

SLOW PROGRESS IN PREPARING TO MEET THE ENEMY

Efforts to Repair Hull's Loss—General Harrison Appointed Commander-in-Chief—Siege of Fort Wayne Relieved—General Winchester Appointed to Succeed Harrison without Cause.

WHEN the critical state of affairs at Detroit was made known to Governor Meigs, he immediately ordered the remaining part of Ohio's quota of the one hundred thousand detached militia, which the President was authorized to levy among the States, twelve hundred in number, to rendezvous under Brigadier-General Tupper at Urbana, which was well in the southern edge of the wilderness. When the Governor learned of the loss of Detroit, he became active in placing every effective force and point in good condition for successful defence against the Savages; also in advising the frontiersmen to gather and build blockhouses for the protection of their families.

Kentucky, under the Governorship of the veteran General Charles Scott, was prompt in gathering her quota of ten regiments of five hundred and fifty men each. Governor Harrison, who, the preceding year, had been commissioned to command the troops in Indiana and Illinois Territories, had, with his characteristic thoughtfulness and good judgment, secured places of refuge for the settlers in his domain. He was also authorized to call on the Governor of Kentucky for any soldiers, needed from that State, which were not in service.

By invitation of Governor Scott, his comrade in General Wayne's campaign through Ohio, Harrison visited Frankfort, inspected the militia, and was given a public reception, the principal citizens including Henry Clay uniting to do him honor; and in order that he might be chief in command of the Kentucky forces, Governor Scott commissioned him, August 25, 1812, Major-General of the militia of Kentucky by brevet. It was not known by either party that President Madison had, on August 22d, commissioned him Brigadier-General in the Army of the United States.

Writing to Governor Meigs from Cincinnati on

the 27th, General Harrison stated, that the Kentucky troops then with him were two regiments of infantry and one of mounted riflemen, which were ordered at once to Urbana; and that three regiments of infantry, one of dragoons, and one of mounted riflemen were in full march to join him—the whole number being over four thousand men. He further stated that "should the report of the capture of General Hull's army prove untrue, I shall join them either at that place [Urbana], or before they reach it, and proceed to Detroit without waiting for the regiments in my rear." He also inquired what assistance could be given him from Ohio.

The Kentucky troops marched up the Miami Valley, and were overtaken by General Harrison the third day. On September 2d, when above Dayton, they were overtaken by an express bearing the United States commission for General Harrison and instructions for him to take command of the Indiana and Illinois troops, and co-operate with General Hull of Detroit, and Governor Howard of Missouri Territory, as General James Winchester had been assigned to the chief command of the Northwestern Army.

The march was continued to Piqua, where they arrived September 3d, to learn that Fort Wayne, which had been rebuilt by Colonel Thomas Hunt in 1804, was strongly besieged by Savages, and that a strong command of British and Savages had been sent from Fort Malden for the conquest of the Maumee and Wabash valleys. The Aborigine Agent at Piqua, Colonel John Johnston, at the request of General Harrison, sent some Shawnee scouts yet on his pay-roll to the site of Fort Defiance, to ascertain if any British force had passed up the Maumee River to the siege of Fort Wayne. Captain John Logan, a friendly and efficient Shawnee half-breed, was sent to Fort Wayne, to learn and to report its condition as soon as possible.

Immediate action seemed imperative, and, without awaiting General Winchester's arrival or his orders, General Harrison ordered Lieutenant-Colonel John Allen's regiment of Federal troops, with two companies from Colonel Lewis's regiment, and one company from Colonel Scott's regiment, to prepare for a forced march to the relief of Fort Wayne.[1]

[1] Early the next day, the 5th September, General Harrison paraded the remainder of the troops and delivered to them a speech, detailing the duties of soldiers, and stating if there was any person who would not submit to such regulations, or who was afraid to risk his life in defence of his country, he might return home. Only one man desired to return; and his friends having obtained leave, as usual,

For the cavalry a delay of two days was necessary, that they might receive flints for their guns, and a few other supplies that were expected daily; and at dawn, on September 6th, they moved briskly forward in light marching order, and, early on the 8th, came up with Colonel Allen's command at St. Marys, where an express from General Harrison had overtaken Colonel Allen, with orders to halt and build a stockaded fort, for the protection of the sick, and security of provisions. Here they were joined by Major Richard M. Johnson, with a corps of Kentucky mounted volunteers. That night, Aborigines were seen spying the encampment, but they did not molest any one. They returned to the besiegers of Fort Wayne with the report that "Kentuck was coming as numerous as the trees." Here, also, the messenger, Captain Logan, reported his observations of the distressed condition of Fort Wayne, he having evaded the besiegers and returned in safety. The afternoon of September 9th, the army encamped at Shane's Crossing of the river St. Marys, the

---

to escort him on his way, he was hoisted on a rail and carried to the Big Miami, in the waters of which they absolved him from the obligations of courage and patriotism, and then gave him leave of absence.—Captain Robert M'Afee's *History of the Late War* (1812), page 121.

From 1812-1813

present Rockford, Ohio, where they met Colonel Adams, with a good force of Ohio volunteer cavalry. From this place the combined forces moved cautiously, and in as near battle order as practicable. General Harrison was a member of General Wayne's staff during his campaign through this wilderness and he had been an apt student of Wayne's successful methods. The encampment was fortified, or well protected each night, and the march by day was in such order as to prevent being ambuscaded. He also kept well informed regarding the condition and temper of each division.

The scouts soon reconnoitered the country around Fort Wayne, and found that the Savages had made good their escape. That afternoon, most of the army encamped near the fort, where a short time before had been a comfortable village. It was now in ruins, having been burned by the Savages, together with the United States Factory (trading agency building) which had been erected to supply the ungrateful wretches with farming utensils and the comforts of civilized life.

British agents were constantly with the Savages, to prevent defection in their bands and activities. At the councils held in the farther West, and nearer, it was reported by the Savages that they had been promised that, if they would besiege the posts, Fort Wayne and Fort Harrison by the Wabash, and prevent their abandonment, as at Fort Dearborn, they should be joined in one moon by a large British force from Forts Malden and Detroit, with artillery, able to demolish the stockades and give the garrisons to massacre and spoil —and their success in this would expose the whole frontier to their devastation. Such report would seem incredible at this day, were it not that such deeds had repeatedly been committed by the British and their savage allies formerly, and that they were done at every one of their successful opportunities during the War of 1812.

As in former wars, an occasional Frenchman was friendly and true to the Americans. Antoine Bondie was such an one at Fort Wayne; and it was evidently through his early warnings and personal influence at critical moments that the garrison was saved from massacre, and the post preserved to the Americans.

The number of savage warriors besieging Fort Wayne was estimated at five hundred; and the garrison numbered about eighty. The Savages were secreted around in every available place, hoping to observe the sentries in thoughtless exposure, or some weak point at the entrance gate or about the stockade. They essayed strategy. They killed Stephen Johnson, clerk in the agency store, who sought to evade them and visit Piqua to look after his wife. They killed the garrison's cattle and hogs, and committed every depredation possible. Both parties wished to delay the final conflict—the Americans awaiting General Harrison's arrival, the Savages and their British helpers that of their promised reinforcements.

Upon the arrival of General Harrison, he reconnoitered the country in all directions, and found that the enemy had retreated toward Malden.

CHAPTER XVIII

EXTREME SUFFERINGS OF KENTUCKY SOLDIERS

General Winchester Assumes Command of the Army—Harrison Directs Clearing of Roads and Building of Forts Barbee, Jennings, and Amanda—Winchester Marches Army from Fort Wayne to Defiance—British Force Checked on their Way to Fort Wayne—Harrison Reappointed Chief in Command of Northwestern Army—Visits Winchester at Defiance and Settles Discord—Plans Fort Winchester which Was Built at Defiance—Extreme Sufferings of Winchester's Left Wing of the Army—Battle of Mississinewa River.

WINCHESTER arrived at Fort Wayne September 19th, and Harrison at once recognized him as his ranking officer, stranger though he was to this wilderness country, to the ways of the Savages, and to the condition of affairs; and a General Order was issued to the soldiers introducing the new commander and urging strict obedience to his commands.

The necessity for additional roads and places for the protection of food and other military supplies being urgent, General Harrison returned to St. Marys, where he found the expected Kentucky troops. Colonel Joshua Barbee was instructed to build there an ample fortification, and storehouse within the stockades, which was named Fort Barbee. Colonel William Jennings was ordered to open a direct road toward Defiance, and to build a fort at the end of the portage by the Auglaize River. This post was named Fort Jennings, which name is perpetuated at its site by a pleasant village with the same name. Colonel Findlay's regiment of Ohio cavalry, which the Governor had ordered to report at St. Marys, was ordered forward to destroy the prominent Ottawa towns by the Blanchard River, their former inhabitants having been hostile and now favoring the British.

General Winchester remained at Fort Wayne two days and, September 22d, "rejoicing in the prospect" of recouping the disaster at Detroit, he moved his army of about two thousand anxious soldiers down the left bank of the Maumee River. The savage scouts of the enemy ambushed and killed several of his scouts, and endeavored to entrap others. It soon developed that the enemy's scouts were the advance line of about two hundred British troops under Major Muir, and one thousand or more Savages led by the notorious Colonel Matthew Elliott. This was the force previously reported as coming from Fort Malden to aid in the reduction of Fort Wayne. They had brought by boats to the site of Fort Defiance four cannon and other heavy equipment, and had then advanced in as near readiness for battle as possible. Upon learning that they would meet a strong force of Americans in front, and that their retreat would be cut off by an oncoming force down the Auglaize River, they hastily retreated the way they had come.

Winchester, fording the Maumee about five miles above the site of Fort Defiance, advanced cautiously down the way of the retreating foe and, on September 30th, fortified an encampment on the right high bank of the Maumee, one mile and a half by river above the site of General Wayne's Fort Defiance.

Meantime, General Harrison had received a letter from the Secretary of War, announcing that he was assigned to the full command of the Northwestern Army, which, in addition to the regular troops and rangers in that quarter, would consist of the volunteers and militia of Kentucky, Ohio, and three thousand men from Virginia and Pennsylvania, making his entire force ten thousand. This desirable appointment of Harrison was due to the influence of his many friends in Kentucky, as well as those north of the Ohio River, who realized the mistake of having Winchester outrank him.

Winchester's report of the enemy was received by Harrison at Fort Barbee September 30th, as was also a report from Governor Meigs of a strong force of the enemy opposing Winchester. The three thousand men then at Fort Barbee were at once started direct for Defiance, Harrison commanding in person. The first night they encamped at Fort Jennings, where word of the retreat of the enemy was received. This gave opportunity for part of the soldiers to clear the road to Defiance, and others to build a fortification farther up the Auglaize River, on the site of Wayne's Fort Auglaize. This post was named by Colonel Pogue, its builder, Fort Amanda, in honor of his wife.

General Harrison, with the cavalry, continued down the river, along the Wayne trace of eighteen years before. Upon his arrival at Winchester's encampment many of the latter's soldiers were found in a condition bordering on revolt. The food supplies had become short, and the men were suffering from insufficient clothing and from sickness. They had been unfavorably impressed with their General. They greeted Harrison, however, with great warmth, and his address to them was received in very good spirit. The food brought with the visitors gave the hungry men a better breakfast than they had been accustomed to, which, together with the parading and fraternizing of the cavalry, renewed the soldierly spirit. New plans were entered upon. They found Wayne's Fort Defiance in ruins; and even had it remained in good condition its size would have been inadequate for the present demands. Harrison selected another site near by, along the high bank of the Auglaize River, and drew a plan for a new fort and stockaded enclosure, to embrace twelve times the ground space, or more, of the former Fort Defiance; and the soldiers began its construction in good spirits. Harrison named this post Fort Winchester.

The Northwestern Army was divided into two wings and a center. General Winchester was directed to retain his command, which was to be known as the left wing. The right wing was composed of the brigades from Virginia and Pennsylvania, and one brigade from southeastern Ohio. This wing proceeded down the Sandusky River, and built Fort Feree at Upper

From 1812-1813

Sandusky, Fort Ball at the present Tiffin, and Fort Stephenson at Lower Sandusky, now Fremont, Ohio. General Tupper was to command the center, moving along Hull's Road by Forts McArthur, Necessity, and Findlay, heretofore mentioned.

While at Defiance, General Harrison discussed with Winchester the lateness of the season; the difficulties of advancing the army during the winter; the food supply; health of the soldiers; and the desirability of his sending two of his regiments southward for the winter, where they would be near the source of supply of food and clothing. They also debated whether General Tupper, with the cavalry, nearly a thousand in number, should be sent down the Maumee beyond the lowest rapids, to disperse any of the enemy there found, thus saving the crops abandoned there by the American settlers; and return to Fort Barbee by way of the Ottawa towns by the Blanchard River. These suggested orders were not decided upon by Winchester and Tupper. There was friction between the commanders, and also between the Federal and volunteer soldiers, which prevented the proposed expedition of the left wing. This wing, Tupper wrote, "was at one time capable of tearing the British flag from the walls of Detroit."

Rumors of Fort Wayne being again besieged, and the activity of the Savages around the workmen while building Fort Winchester, the expiration of the time of enlistment of many men, and particularly the lateness of the season with scarcity of food and clothing, and, withal, much sickness, kept the soldiers from advancing toward Detroit, as had been expected.

During General Winchester's stay, of about three months, just above and below Defiance, his army occupied five encampments, two below being temporary. With continued short rations, delay in the receipt of winter clothing, and the growing severity of the winter, the sickness and sufferings of the soldiers were increasing, and the changes of encampment were made for sanitary reasons, and that the men might be nearer timber for fuel.

On account of their hurried march to the relief of Fort Wayne, much of the soldiers' clothing was left at Piqua, and many of the men were yet wearing the linen hunting coats in which they started from their homes in Kentucky, on 12th August; and these were in rags from natural wear, and from the brush and timber with which they had been obliged to contend. Many were so entirely destitute of shoes and other clothing, that they must have frozen had they been obliged to go much distance from their camp-fires. The "Black Swamp" through which they travelled during the hot weather, and in which they were yet dwelling, was rank with intermittent and remittent fevers which were weakening their systems, and making them susceptible to pneumonia and typhoid fever. The attacks of the latter were facilitated, also, by the fact that the men were huddled together to share each other's warmth, and had only impure surface water to drink. On account of their great distance in the forest, the severe and continued rains, and the soft, miry condition of the swamps, food could not be carried to them in sufficient quantities. Much was lost on the way by not over-conscientious packhorse men; and much that was delivered was in such soiled and spoiled condition as to be unwholesome. At their Camp Number Three, five miles down the Maumee from Defiance, the sufferings and deaths were the worst. No record has been found of the total number of deaths, which were several each day; nor have markings of the places of their scattered and shallow interment been discovered in later years. Captain Robert B. M'Afee, and William Atherton, who were with this army, recount in their small books many other details of the sufferings and deaths of this unfortunate army; probably among the greatest sufferings of their kind that American soldiers have endured.

General Harrison, at this time, had headquarters at Franklinton, now Columbus, Ohio, but was often in the saddle, and kept informed regarding the condition of affairs generally; and he put forth great efforts to gather supplies and men, and to advance them toward Detroit. He found in his work, other than the difficulty of getting supplies forward through a swampy wilderness of nearly two hundred miles, in wagons or on packhorses which were forced to carry their own food also, obstacles which he declared to be "absolutely impossible." Different efforts to reconnoiter the lower Maumee, and to punish the aggressive Savages, were barren of desirable results, while increasing the sufferings of the soldiers.

The greatest loss in battle, during this time, was suffered in December by Lieutenant-Colonel Campbell's expedition from Fort McArthur. This was against the Miami and Delaware bands of Aborigines and extended to the Mississinewa River in Indiana. Here the enemy made sharp opposition, killing eight Americans, and wounding forty-two others; also killing one hundred and seven horses. The enemy left fifteen of their dead on the field. On the return to Ohio, it was necessary to carry the wounded on stretchers, and on the way three hundred of the American soldiers were so frost-bitten as to be unfit for duty for several weeks.

CHAPTER XIX

THE SECOND GREAT DISASTER OF THE WAR OF 1812

Advance of General Winchester's Army from Defiance—Safe Arrival at Presque Isle below Roche de Bout—There Builds Fort Deposit—Unwise Advance of Army to the Raisin—Defeat and Massacre—Harrison Gathers a New Army and Takes Command—Fort Deposit Abandoned—Fort Winchester again the Frontier Post—Fort Meigs Built—Efforts to Strike the Enemy Unavailing.

ON December 22, 1812, flour and other supplies, including a partial supply of clothing, were received in fairly good condition, comparatively, by General Winchester's army in camp near Defiance. Preparations were at once made for the advance of all those able to march. The sick and convalescent were moved to Fort Winchester, and the last days of December, 1812, the stronger soldiers started slowly and wearily down the north bank of the Maumee River, hauling their supplies and equipment by their own reduced power on sleds that had been hastily improvised. A deep snow had recently fallen on wet ground that had been made soft by a general thaw. The march by day was distressful, often through water in the numerous gullies; and worse was the protracted difficulty of getting fire with flint and steel, when all fuel was sodden by rain and melting snow, and the enforced wakefulness from wet clothing and insufficient warmth during the freezing nights.

The army, now reduced to about thirteen hundred men, arrived at Presque Isle, the starting place of Wayne's Battle of Fallen Timber, January 10, 1813. On the near-by lower ground, a cornfield was discovered, which yielded sufficiently for a good change of diet for the hungry and nearly exhausted men, it being relished at first after being hastily boiled whole, mature and hard as it was. Here an encampment was planned, and fortified to some extent, and a large storehouse for provisions and heavy baggage, to be received, was built within the stockades. The receipt of additional supplies, including clothing, with the warmer camp, soon revived the soldierly spirit.

Reports to, and orders from, General Harrison were delayed in transit. This advance and occupation of the lower rapids of the Maumee by Winchester without opposition by the enemy was reassuring to the officers and to the ranks; and this had much influence in inducing an unwise advance to the river Raisin.

In compliance with several requests for protection received from Frenchtown (now Monroe, Michigan, then a settlement of thirty-three families), Colonel William Lewis, with five hundred and fifty soldiers, was dispatched January 17th for that purpose, by General Winchester. A few hours later, Colonel John Allen followed with a force of one hundred and ten men which overtook the former opposite Presque Isle of Maumee Bay, where they were informed that there were four hundred Aborigines then at Frenchtown, and that Colonel Elliott was detaching a force at Fort Malden to proceed against the Americans by the Maumee River. These rumors were dispatched to General Winchester, and he sent them to General Harrison, together with a statement of the movement of his main force against the enemy.

Colonels Lewis and Allen rapidly advanced over the ice along the shore of Lake Erie, engaged the enemy, about one hundred British troops and four hundred Aborigines, near Frenchtown, and drove them across the river Raisin, notwithstanding the opposing howitzer. Winchester's officers then dispatched for reinforcements, and began preparations for defence against oncoming superior numbers.

Upon learning of the success of his colonels, Winchester left a guard at his Fort Deposit, and started January 19th, with all his remaining force, two hundred and fifty in number, for Frenchtown, where he arrived in the night of the 20th. He established head-quarters in the comfortable residence of Colonel Francis Navarre, on the south side of the river, about nine hundred feet from the camp of his soldiers. The next day, he was informed by Peter Navarre and his four brothers, whom he sent out to reconnoiter, that a large force of British and Aborigines from Fort Malden, about twenty-five miles distant, would attack that night. Counter advices, less trustworthy, prevailed, however, and no definite precautions against a night attack were ordered.

Very early in the morning of the 22d, the brave American troops, still weak from their former scant rations, disease, and marchings, were surprised by the stealthy foe, and were quite overwhelmed by superior numbers supported by six cannon. In the first onslaught, and in the later direct massacre, and by the burning of the buildings in which the wounded were placed, about three hundred were killed; five hundred and forty-seven were taken prisoners by the British and forty-five by the Aborigines; and only thirty-three escaped.

Winchester, aroused by the guns, strove in the biting cold to join his men. Mounting his host's horse he rode in the direction he supposed to be the proper part of their camp. He was soon captured by Jack Brandy, an Aborigine of Round Head's band, who divested him of his outer clothing, and led him half frozen to Colonel Proctor, the British commander, who persuaded him to order the surrender of his troops. The white flag was started with this order towards the garden pickets, behind which the Americans were well holding their position. They refused to surrender. Three times did the flag pass from the British head-quarters to the American line, once accompanied by Major Overton of Winchester's staff, before the courageous Major George Madison would surrender; and he then consented only after promises by Proctor of protection from the Savages. How these promises were ignored by the British, in the case of the many soldiers wounded, and captured by the

Savages; and how fully the intoxicated Savages revelled in the butchery and eating of their helpless victims, leaving the remains to be eaten by dogs and hogs, has been described by many persons whose writings are readily accessible.

Most of the American prisoners who could march with the British were led to Fort Malden the morning of the 23d. On the 26th, they were marched to Sandwich, whence some were sent across the river to Detroit, and the others to Fort George at Niagara, where nearly all of them were released on parole "not to bear arms against his Majesty or his allies [the Savages] during the war or until exchanged." Winchester, Lewis, and Madison were sent to Quebec and, sometime later, to Beauport where they were confined until the spring of 1814, when they were exchanged with many others.

Colonel Proctor reported the British loss in this battle as twenty-four killed and one hundred and fifty-eight wounded. No accurate estimate of the loss of their allied Savages could be made. The enemy numbered about two thousand, one half being British regulars and Canadian militia. Round Head and Walk-in-the-Water were the principal chiefs of the Savages. Tecumseh was then in Indiana. Proctor's report and commendation of his Savage "allies" led the Assembly of Lower Canada to extend to him "and his men" a vote of thanks; and the part he acted also led to his promotion to the rank of Brigadier-General.

This great disaster at the river Raisin, though most deeply lamented, was not without good results in its lessons. "Remember the Raisin" became the slogan that decided many other men, as well as Kentuckians, to enlist in the army, and to do valiant service for their country; and it also stimulated the officers to greater thoughtfulness, and to a greater sense of responsibility.

General Harrison, at Upper Sandusky, upon receipt of Winchester's report that he was advancing to the Raisin, urged forward troops and artillery from his head-quarters, and from Lower Sandusky. He preceded the troops and, upon his arrival at Fort Deposit, ordered forward General Payne, with the garrison there, to the support of their General. The cold was severe, the snow-covered road was rough, and miry in places, and Harrison's troops were slow in arriving at the lower rapids. As they arrived in small bodies, they were hastened onward toward the Raisin, led by General Harrison in person. They had not proceeded far, however, before some fugitives were met who gave the sad report; and farther advancement confirmed the total defeat of Winchester's command. A council of officers in the saddle decided to send scouts forward to aid those escaping, and to return all other of the scattered small bands to Fort Deposit.

It was here decided that this fort's position was untenable against any formidable force; and the troops set fire to the blockhouse the next morning and abandoned the fortification. They retired to the Portage River, about eighteen miles eastward on the road to Lower Sandusky, where they strongly fortified an encampment, and awaited the oncoming regiments and artillery. Copious rains ensued and delayed forward movements.

Fort Winchester again became the frontier position of defence in the Maumee Valley, and a shield to the forts and the settlers to the south and southwest, who were again experiencing great alarm.

Scouts from the Portage River kept the movements of the Savages under observation. On February 9th they reported that about six hundred were gathered on the north shore of Maumee Bay. Harrison detached six hundred soldiers with one cannon, and led them in person to the

Savage encampment, which was abandoned by the enemy on approach of the Americans. They were pursued, but effected safe escape to Fort Malden.

Harrison's experience with Wayne along the lower Maumee, and his later observations, led him to choose the site for the fort he had decided to build, on the high right bank of the Maumee, a short distance below the lowest fording place, and near the foot of the lowest rapids; this site being across the ravine adjoining (above) the present village of Perrysburg, Ohio. The plan was agreed upon with Captain Wood, chief engineer, to embrace eight blockhouses with double timbers, four large batteries, and a fortified encampment twenty-five hundred yards in circumference, the lines being irregular on account of the slopings of the land. This fortification was begun early in February and its completion was delayed by the weather, sickness, and the heavy work necessary. As it approached completion, it was given the name Fort Meigs, in honor of Ohio's patriotic and efficient Governor.

Late in February, ice formed around the armed British vessels at Fort Malden, and a bold plan for their destruction was entered upon; to be frustrated, however, by the weakening courage of some of the party and by the thawing of the ice.

The oversight of everything devolved upon General Harrison. Soon after the favorable beginning of Fort Meigs, he started southward to urge forward additional troops in person, and to visit his sick family at Cincinnati. Captain Wood had been sent by him to Lower Sandusky to plan a fortification for that place. General Leftwich of the Virginia militia, whom Captain Wood afterwards called "an old phlegmatic Dutchman who was not even fit for a packhorse master, much less to be entrusted with such an important command" as this, was left in charge of the camp and the building of the fort. He permitted the work to cease, and, further, permitted the soldiers to use the gathered timber for fuel while there was within easy distance much better material for such use, the clearing away of which was necessary. Captain Wood returned the 20th of February to find, also, that there had been considerable destruction of the work that was done before his departure.

The time of enlistment of the Virginians, and some Pennsylvanians, soon expired, and they started for home, leaving only about five hundred soldiers at this important encampment. However, work was resumed with spirit, and the encampment limits were extended to embrace fourteen acres or more of land, for the purpose of encompassing and protecting, in case of being besieged, the entire army, horses, cattle, wagons, and supplies which were to be centered here.

CHAPTER XX

A THIRD GREAT DISASTER IN THE FIRST YEAR OF THE WAR

The Northwestern Army Neglected by the General Government—General Harrison not Distracted by Unwise Advisers—Investment and Siege of Fort Meigs—Reinforcements for the Fort Disobey Orders—They are Surrounded and Captured—Further Massacre and Cannibalism by British Allies—The Enemy Raises Siege and Retreats.

ABOUT the first of March, 1813, a small party of citizens of Detroit arrived at Fort Meigs, and reported that General Proctor had ordered the assembling of Canadian militia on the 7th of April at Sandwich, preparatory for an attack on Fort Meigs; and the mode of attack, as discussed by the British officers, was to be by constructing strong batteries of their heaviest cannon on the opposite side of the Maumee to be manned by British artillerymen, while the Savages were to invest the fort on other sides. In the opinion of Major Muir "a few hours' action of the cannon would smoke the Americans out of the Fort into the hands of the Savages." Many other boastings were reported.

British scouts of all kinds continued active in the vicinity of Fort Meigs, and hunting for game by Americans near by became dangerous. Lieutenant Walker exposed himself to, and was killed by them.

The Northwestern Army was being neglected by Eastern authorities. General Harrison found it impossible to get the number and character of troops he thought necessary for the work to be done. Evil advisers, also, annoyed him, and distracted others, by their urging him to scatter his insufficient forces; to increase his work beyond the ability of his number to perform; and to change his base of operations to a less important point, which would leave the most desirable part of the country open to the enemy. But the General, by his indefatigable energies, succeeded in carrying out his desires, excepting in the number of soldiers. The fortunate rising of the rivers facilitated the receipt of food supplies by boats.

The gathering of the Savages, Canadian militia, and British regular troops, according to the agreement of officers before reported, was observed and reported to Harrison. Fort Meigs was strengthened, and supplied, to withstand the combined attack that was threatened and now appeared inevitable and imminent. Fortunately the Savages of the West and Southwest were massed with the British, very few being left to continue their raids on the frontier settlements.

On April 28, 1813, the British army landed from numerous boats near the ruins of their former Fort Miami, about two miles below, and on the opposite (left) bank of the Maumee from Fort Meigs, where they made and continued their principal encampment on the high ground. The Americans were powerless to oppose this action, as the Savages had been gathering in force around the fort, and soon had it thoroughly invested.

There had been continuous rain, and the efforts of the British to move their heavy cannon, and construct batteries, were very laborious and attended with delays. The work was carried forward first only at night, and later uninterruptedly day and night with strong relays, notwithstanding the rain, and shots from Fort Meigs which killed and wounded some of their men. Cannon were also taken across the river to support the Savages, who were meeting with warm opposition by the garrison. Meantime high traverses of earth were being thrown up by the garrison, to protect the Americans from shots of the enemy from all directions; also underground resting places for the troops, and refuges from bombs.

On the early morning of April 30th, the enemy had completed two batteries nearly opposite Fort Meigs, one battery of two twenty-four-pounder cannon (the heaviest at the fort being two eighteen-pounders) and the other of three howitzers, one eight inches and the other two five and a half inches calibre. Their fire became constant. The enemy completed a third battery of three twelve-pounder cannon the night of May 1st, between the other two; also on the 3d of May a battery of several mortars was put in operation by them nearer the river. After a few well directed shots from the fort, the cannon in the ravine to the eastward were moved to a greater range. The strong batteries on the opposite side of the river, however, continued rapid and carefully directed firing.

On May 4th, General Proctor sent his Major Chalmers with a white flag to demand surrender of the fort. General Harrison promptly replied: "Tell General Proctor that if he shall take the Fort it will be under circumstances that will do him more honor than a thousand surrenders."

That night, about 11 o'clock, Harrison's anxiety regarding the expected reinforcements was largely relieved by the return of his messenger Captain Oliver, accompanied by Major David Trimble and fifteen soldiers who had evaded the Savages. They reported that General Green Clay's command, eleven hundred in number, in eighteen large flatboats with high sides to protect the soldiers from the fire of what Savages they might meet, were at the left bank of the Maumee at the head of the Grand Rapids, fourteen miles above, the river being so high that the pilot declined to run the rapids in such a dark night unless commanded so to do.

Captain Hamilton was dispatched to meet General Clay, with orders to detach about eight hundred men, land them early in the morning at a designated point a little above the fort, capture the British batteries, spike the guns, and come at once to the fort.

Colonel William Dudley was chosen by General Clay for this important work. He and his courageous soldiers succeeded in landing well and in capturing the guns; but, being desirous to inflict punishment upon a band of Savages that had opened fire upon them, they forgot the imperative orders to cross immediately to the fort, and pursued the Savages, who led them away from the river to be surrounded by overwhelming numbers. Of his eight hundred and sixty men, only one hundred and seventy escaped to the fort. Many were killed, including Colonel Dudley, in the fierce contest that continued about three hours. Many others were wounded, scalped, and stripped of clothing by the Savages. Those who were captured, and could walk, were started for the ruins of the British Fort Miami near the enemy's encampment.

Although now under direct command of the British, many were slain by the Savages while on this march; and the stripping of Americans, dead and alive, of their clothing and other possessions was freely indulged. At Fort Miami, the prisoners were compelled by the Savages to run the gauntlet, where many more were killed by the British allies with war clubs, scalping knives, tomahawks, and pistols. Major Richardson, of the 41st British Regiment, wrote that forty of these prisoners were thus killed before the others could be taken on board the gunboats. He continues:

"On the evening of the second day after this event I accompanied Major Muir, of the 41st, in a ramble throughout the encampment of the Indians, distant some few hundred yards from our own. The spectacle there offered to our view was at once of the most ludicrous and revolting nature. In various directions were lying the trunks and boxes taken from the boats of the American division, and the plunderers were busily occupied in displaying their riches, carefully examining each article, and attempting to define its use. Several were decked out in the uniforms of officers; and although embarrassed to the last degree in their movements, and dragging with difficulty the heavy military boots with which their legs were for the first time covered, strutted forth much to the admiration of their less fortunate comrades. Some were habited in plain clothes; others had their bodies clad with clean white shirts, contrasting in no ordinary manner with the swarthiness of their skins; all wore some articles of decoration, and their tents were ornamented with saddles, bridles, rifles, daggers, swords and pistols, many of which were handsomely mounted and of curious workmanship. Such was the ridiculous part of the picture.

"But, mingled with these in various directions, were to be seen the scalps of the slain drying in the sun, stained on the flesh side with vermilion dyes, and dangling in air as they hung suspended from poles to which they were attached, together with hoops of various sizes on which were stretched portions of human skin taken from various parts of the human body, principally the hand and foot and yet covered with the nails of those parts; while scattered along the ground were visible the members from which they had been separated, and which were serving as nutriment to the wolf-dogs by which the Savages were accompanied.

"As we continued to advance into the heart of the encampment a scene of a more disgusting nature arrested our attention. Stopping at the entrance of a tent occupied by the Minoumini [Menomeni] tribe we observed them seated around a large fire over which was suspended a kettle containing their meal. Each warrior had a piece of string hanging over the edge of the vessel, and to this was suspended a food which, it will be presumed we heard not without loathing, consisted of a part of an American. Any expression of our feelings, as we declined the invitation they gave us to join in their repast, would have been resented by the Savages without ceremony [sic]; we had, therefore, the prudence to excuse ourselves under the plea that we had already taken our food, and we hastened to remove from a sight so revolting to humanity."

The 5th of May, 1813, was a sad day at Fort Meigs on account of this, the third great loss suffered by the Army of the Northwest in less than one year after the beginning of the War of 1812.

General Harrison, from his outlook, saw the beginning of the fatal error of Colonel Dudley's doomed troops. He signalled, repeating his former command to come at once to the fort, but his signals were lost to the enthusiastic men, "whose excessive ardor . . . always the case when Kentucky militia were engaged . . . was the source of all their misfortunes." A volunteer was called for, to convey to Colonel Dudley the imperative command of the General to retreat to the fort. Lieutenant Campbell responded; but he arrived near the farther shore too late.

The other troops of General Clay's command became separated in their efforts to land from the rapid current, but, with the aid of a sortie sent out by General Harrison, fought their way to the fort through the Savages on the right bank of the river.

The spiking of eleven of the British cannon by Dudley's command was done, from want of anything better, with ramrods of their small guns. These rods were readily removed by the British gunners, who then with them began again a vigorous fire upon the fort.

The American supply of balls and shells for their twelve- and eighteen-pounder cannon was small, and these guns answered those of the British only occasionally and to the best advantage. To increase the supply a gill of whiskey was offered the soldiers for every British ball that could be found of these sizes and delivered to the keeper of the magazine.

The free license given the Savages in their butcheries and cannibalism of Colonel Dudley and his brave men sated them, and they began to desert their allies, the British. Proctor again sent a white flag to demand surrender of the fort. The reply was such as to indicate that the demand was considered an insult by Harrison; and upon its receipt the enemy began preparations to raise the siege. The efforts to remove the siege guns were made dangerous and delayed by the American cannon, although the British gunboats were sent as near Fort Meigs as practicable to divert attention.

As part of his report to Governor Sir George Prevost, Proctor wrote:

"I had not the option of retaining my position on the Miami [Maumee]. Half of the militia had left us.... Before the ordnance could be withdrawn from batteries I was left with Tecumseh and less than twenty chiefs and warriors—a circumstance which strongly proves that, under present circumstances at least, our Indian force is not a disposable one, or permanent, though occasionally a most powerful aid."

Governor Prevost reported to his superior that the battles on the Maumee "terminated in the complete defeat of the enemy, and capture, dispersion, or destruction of thirteen hundred men." The British loss was reported as fifteen killed, forty-seven wounded, and forty-four taken prisoners. The loss of the Savages was far greater, but, as usual, the number was impossible to obtain. The American loss was eighty-one killed and one hundred and eighty-nine wounded, of which number seventeen were killed and sixty-five wounded within the fortified enclosure. The Savages took away between thirty and forty American prisoners, mostly of Dudley's defeated command.

On May 9th, immediately after the departure of the enemy, General Harrison sent out a detachment to gather all the bodies of the killed they could find. The indifference of the British in their nominal burying of the dead of Colonel Dudley's command, in contradiction of Major Richardson's statement, was shown by finding fragments of forty-five Kentuckians, which the Americans conveyed across the river, and buried with the honors of war in the fort's cemetery.

CHAPTER XXI

SECOND GREAT EFFORT OF THE ENEMY UNAVAILING

The British Gather More Savage Allies—More Preparations by Americans for Advancing upon the Enemy—Celebration of Fourth of July by Soldiers in the Forest—The Enemy Becoming More Active—Fort Seneca Built to Retain Friendship of Aged Aborigines—Second Investment of Fort Meigs by Increased Force—Scheme for its Capture Unavailing—Second Retreat of Enemy from Fort Meigs.

PROCTOR made a proposition to exchange his American prisoners for the Aborigines of the frontiers, aged and infirm men, who were not prisoners of, or hostile against, the United States. Of course such proposition could not be entertained; but Harrison replied that he would refer it to the President.

Tecumseh's and Proctor's emissaries to the more distant tribes of Aborigines had gathered large numbers of them, and, in June, 1813, more than one thousand of the most savage and depraved were marched by their chiefs and a Scotch trader, Dickson, from their rendezvous at Chicago to Fort Malden. Colonel Richard M. Johnson, who had left Congress and organized a regiment of seven hundred mounted Kentuckians, was directed to move around the headwaters of the Auglaize and Maumee. About the time of the passing of the western Savages through southern Michigan, Colonel Johnson was circulating through northern Indiana, meeting and dispersing Savages near Fort Wayne and to the northwest; but he did not learn of his nearness to the route of the western British reinforcements until later, and far distant.

Meantime supplies were being hastened forward with good success, and stored at Fort Winchester and other posts convenient for distribution to the army which was being prepared for advancing against the enemy. Harrison, who was at Franklinton (now Columbus, Ohio), hastening forward this work, received an express from General Clay at Fort Meigs, informing him that a Frenchman whom the British captured at Dudley's defeat had escaped from Fort Malden and informed him (Clay) that Proctor was about to make a second attack on Fort Meigs with an increased force;

and that he (Clay) had ordered to Fort Meigs Colonel Johnson's command, then at Fort Winchester after guarding boatloads of supplies from Forts Barbee, Wayne, and Amanda.

Johnson, upon receiving Clay's dispatch in the afternoon, although his horses were all much worn, and some disabled, by their continuous marchings, gave orders for the march down the Maumee, and, within half an hour, most of the force began to ford the river just above Fort Winchester point, leaving with the garrison those unable to march. The provisions and baggage in the boats soon followed the cavalcade, and all stopped for the night at General Winchester's Camp Number Three. Early next morning, the march was resumed, and they arrived at Grand Rapids at five o'clock that evening. Here another dispatch was received from General Clay cautioning against ambuscade by Savages who were lying in wait by their route. This information was communicated to the soldiers, who seconded the proposal to proceed, notwithstanding the enemy. A guard was left at Grand Rapids with the boats, which were to continue the journey at daylight the next morning, the main body resuming the march, and, without serious interruption, arriving opposite Fort Meigs at ten o'clock, where they encamped for the night. The fort's daylight gun so frightened the horses that they bolted through the camp, over several of the soldiers, hurting them severely, and continued to run down the river for a half-mile or more, being caught after much trouble and risk. About ten o'clock, the command resumed the march, and, passing above the foot of the lowest rapids, forded the Maumee and encamped just above the stockade of Fort Meigs.

Fort Meigs, itself, was now in better condition for defence than at the time of its siege. The damages done by the British guns had been repaired, and the walls strengthened; the trees, logs, and stumps had been cleared away for a greater distance, and the British battery mounds levelled. Better drainage and sanitary conveniences had also been established. Notwithstanding this improvement, however, the garrison had suffered much sickness, and, during June and July, intermittent and virulent remittent fevers prevailed, which, with dysentery and other complications, proved largely fatal. There were several deaths each day in the small garrison, the aggregate being over one hundred in a period of six weeks.

The 24th Regiment United States Infantry

under Colonel Anderson, from Upper Sandusky, Captain George Croghan with part of the 17th Regiment, and Colonel Ball with his squad of cavalry were all hurried forward.

After ordering these movements by express, General Harrison started northward, and, upon overtaking Colonel Anderson in the evening of June 26th, and learning that Savages were gathering below Fort Meigs, detached three hundred soldiers to make forced march there. Finding quiet prevailing to the eastward along Lake Erie, Harrison proceeded to Fort Meigs, where he arrived the 28th, to find that Johnson also had arrived. Johnson was ordered to detach one hundred and fifty from his command, and to reconnoitre the country to the river Raisin, which was done without discovering much force of the enemy; but this march temporarily thwarted the designs of a force of Savages which had been fitted out from Fort Malden to harass the Americans wherever possible.

The extent of frontier under the surveillance of General Harrison was great; and it required constant watchfulness and great executive ability to guard against invasion, and to gather, and keep, the means and men for the desired advance against the watchful and numerous enemy.

On the 1st of July the General again went eastward, to arrange the defences and garrisons along the Lake to the Cuyahoga River. He directed Colonel Johnson to take post at the Huron River, in northern Ohio. On Johnson's way thither he arrived on the 4th of July at Fort Stephenson, where the few soldiers composing that garrison were celebrating the National Holiday, and, upon their urgent request, he delivered an address that roused their patriotism to a high pitch.

At Fort Meigs, also, there was a grateful celebration of this anniversary day by firing the National Salute; by liberating those who had been imprisoned by court-martial; and by increase of rations. And so it was at all the posts of the Northwestern Army. Thus, throughout the forest, the hearts of the soldiers were cheered, and they were made more contented with their condition by these simple yet effective wilderness celebrations which gave a renewed and a broader significance to their service to their country.

The term of enlistment of some of the garrison of Fort Meigs having expired, and they not being willing to continue their service, a little diversion was planned to start them homeward with good cheer. General Clay, therefore, issued the following General Order, dated July 8th, viz.:

"The commanding General directs that, the Old Guard, on being released, will march out of camp and discharge their guns at a target placed in some secure position; and as a reward for those who may excel in shooting, eight gills of whiskey will be given to the nearest shot, and four gills to the second. The officer of the guard will cause a return, signed for that purpose, signifying the names of the men entitled to the reward."

The Savages were becoming more numerous and troublesome along the Maumee River. Fourteen soldiers whose term of enlistment had expired at Fort Meigs desired to return home by way of Fort Winchester. They were attacked by Savages early on their journey, and but two escaped. Escorts of supply boats were attacked; but they inflicted injury upon the enemy.

Harrison again held council with what Delaware, Seneca, Shawnee, and Wyandot aged non-combatants remained accessible to him, some of them being reported as desirous of going to the British. In order to more fully stimulate and guard their constancy to the United States, he established headquarters at the Seneca town, by the Sandusky River, nine miles above Lower

1813   251

Sandusky (now Fremont, Ohio) and nine miles below Fort Ball, on the site of the present Tiffin; and at this Seneca town he built Fort Seneca during the middle and latter part of July, 1813.

On July 20th, General Proctor, with an army estimated to number at least five thousand, arrived at the mouth of the Maumee River for his second threatened investment of Fort Meigs twelve miles above; and the next morning a picket guard of a corporal and ten soldiers about three hundred yards from Fort Meigs were surprised by Savages, and all but three were killed or captured. The number of Savages now with the British was evidently greater than they had ever before marshalled; and it was probably one of the greatest collections of such warriors ever assembled in America for war—the number being variously estimated at from two to four thousand. M'Afee records the number of warriors as about two thousand and five hundred, and the number of Aborigines fed each day by the British at this time from Malden (now Amherstburg) as seven thousand, including the women and children. It was also reported that there were with the regulars and militia from Malden, one thousand British regulars from Niagara. Undoubtedly efforts had been put forth to gather sufficient force, in their estimation, to crush the United States barriers between them and the liberty of the country west of the Allegheny Mountains. The Savage allies of the British were numerously investing Fort Meigs. They succeeded in capturing some horses and oxen, but their shots were not effective on the garrison, while meeting losses themselves.

Soon after midnight, Lieutenant Montjoy with twenty United States troops arrived at the fort from the Portage River blockhouse, having escaped the Savages with the loss of one man.

General Clay had sent Captain McCune of the Ohio militia to inform General Harrison of the approach of the enemy. This messenger was returned to the fort to report that reinforcements would soon be forthcoming; and Harrison again suggested renewed caution to guard against being surprised.

Lieutenant-Colonel George Paul, with his United States Infantry, and Colonel Ball, with his dragoons, together numbering four hundred and fifty, were ordered forward; also Brigadier-Generals McArthur and Cass (who had recently been promoted) with their Ohio troops. Five hundred additional United States troops were approaching from Fort Massac under Colonel

Theodore Dye Owings (Owens?). These, with the one hundred and forty regulars who were building Fort Seneca, and those at Forts Stephenson and Meigs, would have been a sufficient number, perhaps, for the defence of these posts, had the distant commands been near.

General Clay presented a bold front. On July 23d, he sent Captain McCune with the report that about eight hundred Savages were passing up the opposite (left) bank of the Maumee, possibly to attack Fort Winchester. Harrison believed, correctly, that this movement was only a feint, but, after a council with his staff, scouts were sent out; and McCune was sent back to the fort with this information, and with further precautionary suggestions regarding the wily enemy. The sequel proved the wisdom of the Commander-in-Chief.

Accompanied by James Doolan, a French-Irish Canadian, McCune arrived near Fort Meigs about daybreak, they having lost their way in the night. At the edge of the fort's clearing they were beset by Savages, who were also on horseback, and they were pursued several miles up the river; but here, again, the prowess of the American backwoodsmen outwitted the Savages. They arrived in the fort safely, to report that no more troops could be spared until further arrival from those distant, when Harrison would march to the support of the fort if necessary.

The evening of July 24th, Colonel Gaines with two hundred soldiers made, from Fort Meigs, a detour of the edge of the woods, to reconnoitre the enemy and any batteries they might be constructing. A stronger detachment from the British encampment was started to intercept the return of the Americans, but it did not arrive in time for an engagement. The British moved their main force to the right bank of the river on the 25th, but did not approach within good range of the fort's cannon.

Proctor and Tecumseh had formulated an ingenious strategic plan for the capture of Fort Meigs at night, with little destruction of life to their commands. The British secreted themselves in the deep ravine near the fort to the eastward. Tecumseh, with a large number of Savages, opened a brisk sham battle along the road to Lower Sandusky, as near the fort as practicable, to make it appear to the garrison that they were attacking an American force coming to reinforce the fort. This ruse was for the purpose of drawing part of the garrison from the fort, to allow the British, as with Colonel Dudley's command, to cut off their return, and leave them to be surrounded and massacred by the horde of Savages, while the British would enter the gates under cover of the darkness, take the garrison by surprise, and thus capture the fort. Many soldiers of the garrison desired to sally forth and succor their supposed hard-pressed comrades, but the firmness of General Clay, supported by the memory of repeated cautionings of his Commander-in-Chief, prevailed. Rain, and several discharges of cannon in the fort, soon put a stop to the sham battle.[1]

Remembering their past experience in the spring, and noting that the fort was in better condition to withstand their attack than formerly, the British departed from Fort Meigs, July 27th, without further effort to mislead or capture it; having been in its vicinity about thirty hours.

[1] *See* account of this ruse by the British Major Richardson in the London *New Monthly Magazine* for December, 1826.

CHAPTER XXII

ANOTHER SIGNAL REPULSE OF THE ALLIED ENEMY

British Surround and Attack Fort Stephenson—They are Brilliantly Repulsed by Captain Croghan—They again Retreat to Fort Malden.

AFTER retreating from Fort Meigs the second time, a good part of the British force sailed around through Lake Erie, through Sandusky Bay, and up Sandusky River, to Fort Stephenson, expecting to find it an easy prey. Upon their arrival they found it already invested by their allies, the Savages, who had marched across from Fort Meigs.

Here was another illustration of the good grasp of the general situation, and of the excellent judgment displayed by General Harrison. He did not expect, nor fear, that the enemy would expend much more effort for the capture of Fort Meigs, but he did expect them to direct their energies to his defences of the right wing which possessed large stores, and were not so strongly fortified.

Their investment of Fort Stephenson the first and second days of August, and their repulse by that garrison of but one hundred and sixty men with but one small cannon, under command of the brilliant, young (about twenty-one years of age), courageous, and most patriotic Captain (afterwards Major) George Croghan, nephew of General William Clark, is one of the most remarkable events in the War of 1812. It was preposterous to presume that such small garrison in such weak fortification could withstand such a large, well-equipped, and experienced investing force; hence General Harrison had ordered young Croghan to burn the small amount of stores with the fort and take the garrison to Fort Seneca if the enemy approached. But Captain Croghan was surrounded by Savages before the British appeared, and he, and his garrison, preferred to die at their posts, if die they must, rather than be massacred by the Savages in an effort to escape. This determination, and their alertness, with good judgment in taking advantage of every opportunity, led to one of the most brilliant victories of American arms, with the loss of but one man killed and seven slightly wounded, while inflicting a loss on the enemy of one hundred and twenty.

Late in the afternoon of August 1st, the British gunboats and troops came through Sandusky Bay and up Sandusky River to within sight of Fort Stephenson. They had made sure against retreat of the garrison, and to intercept reinforcements. Captain Croghan was summoned to surrender, but he replied that he and the garrison were determined to defend the fort. After some parleying by the British, with efforts to intimidate, their cannon and howitzers for twenty-four hours threw balls and shells; with little effect, however, until they concentrated on the northwest angle of the fort, evidently to form a breach for assault. The effect of their shot was here guarded against to some extent by bags of sand and sacks of flour being piled against the stockade. The single six-pounder cannon in the fort was fired only at long intervals on account of the scanty supply of ammunition.

Toward the evening of August 2d an assailing party of the British advanced in the direction expected, and to command which the only cannon had been placed, masked, and doubly charged with slugs and grape-shot. At an opportune moment, when the first column of the enemy had advanced into the ditch within ten or fifteen paces of the six-pounder, the masked port was opened and the cannon discharged with dire effect. The second column, that advanced to take the place of their fallen comrades, soon met great loss and confusion from the small arms of the garrison, which completed the disastrous work of the defence in this quarter. The remnant of the assailing columns retreated precipitately and in confusion. Two hundred grenadiers, who were to assail the south side of the fort, did not attain their position until later. They were so warmly opposed by the small arms of the garrison that they soon withdrew.

During the night, which was now come, General Proctor sent Savages to gather the wounded and dead, which they did with those without the range of the garrison's muskets in the darkness. About daylight the British and their savage allies departed from the river and bay, leaving a small vessel containing clothing and military stores, their retreat being hastened by reports of rallying Americans from Fort Seneca.

The garrison supplied the wounded enemy with water, at first in pails let down outside the stockade, and later through an opening made under two stockade timbers, through which the wounded were singly taken within the enclosure and well cared for. The British left behind of their dead, three officers and twenty-five privates; and of their wounded, twenty-six who were taken prisoners.

Scouts were sent early in the morning down the river and bay; but no enemy was discovered other than a few straggling British soldiers who were surprised and captured by the Wyandot Aborigine scouts, recently admitted to the American army, who quickly delivered them at headquarters. These prisoners evidently expected to be massacred like the American prisoners captured by the British allies; and their trepidation and anxiety produced much merriment among their captors, who enjoyed the recollection of it for a long time.

General Proctor sent his army surgeon, Banner, to Fort Stephenson to inquire after his wounded soldiers. This messenger was treated courteously and given every opportunity for personal examination; which was in great contrast to the treatment by the British of Surgeon McKeehan of the Ohio militia, who was sent by General Harrison to Amherstburg, January 31, 1813, to inquire after the wounded of General Winchester's army, following the sad defeat and massacre at the river

Raisin. After receiving much discourteous treatment, Surgeon McKeehan was arrested by order of Proctor and sent to a dungeon at Montreal.

Harrison was informed that many of the Savages with the British were discouraged and dissatisfied with the war after their failures at Fort Meigs and their repulse at Fort Stephenson. He therefore sent to them at Brownstown, below Detroit, some of his most confidential Wyandot chiefs, to confer with Chief Walk-in-the-Water, and the Wyandot warriors under him, for the purpose of spreading the disaffection toward the British, and to secure their neutrality. Such were the alertness and discipline of the British, however, that Colonel McKee and Captain Elliott were at once notified of the visit and were present to prevent or neutralize the proposition. Thereupon the British renewed their work among the Aborigines, extending it to the neutrals by the headwaters of the Auglaize River, the St. Marys, and the Miami to the southward.

The signal success of Captain Croghan at Fort Stephenson ended the invasion of Ohio by the British. General Harrison renewed his efforts to carry the war into the enemy's country; and these efforts soon resulted in driving the British from western Ontario.

CHAPTER XXIII

THE ENTIRE FORCE OF THE BRITISH ON LAKE ERIE CAPTURED

Renewed Efforts for Squadron of Armed Vessels Successful—Oliver H. Perry Builder and Commander—His Difficulties—He Sails for the Enemy—Communicates with Harrison—Meets and Captures All of the British Squadron—Perry's Despatches after the Battle—The Killed and Wounded—Description of Squadrons.

THE early suggestions of General Hull for a United States fleet or squadron of armed vessels on Lake Erie were reported upon favorably, and, in the spring of 1812, Commodore Stewart took action for this purpose. There was, however, but little result from this effort. In September, 1812, Lieutenant Jesse D. Elliott was sent to Black Rock, now part of the city of Buffalo, for the purpose of building such vessels.

On October 8th two armed vessels, the *Detroit* and *Caledonia*, arrived from the British at Detroit, and anchored under the guns of Fort Erie, across the Niagara River from, and a little above Black Rock. Lieutenant Elliott planned their capture at night, and, with the aid of Lieutenant-Colonel (afterward General) Winfield Scott, he succeeded, after a series of remarkable experiences and narrow escapes. The *Detroit* was partly built by General Hull, and went to the British with his surrender of the fort at Detroit; and her first name, *Adams*, was changed by her captors. The British rallied in such force, and so persistently, from Fort Erie to her relief against Lieutenant Elliott's attack and capture, that the Americans burned her on the Niagara River to prevent her recapture. They were more successful in getting the *Caledonia* away from the British. Little was accomplished on new vessels, however.

General Harrison had urged the building of vessels sufficient to cope with the increasing British squadron. This work was seriously undertaken in the spring of 1813 under the direction of Commodore Isaac Chauncey. This officer settled upon Master-Commander Oliver Hazard Perry, of Newport, Rhode Island, to produce the desired squadron. Erie, Pennsylvania, the historic Presque Isle, had been selected as the place of rendezvous, and Commander Perry arrived there for the work March 27, 1813. The work, already well begun, now progressed rapidly.

The British Fort George, by the Niagara River, was captured on May 27th, Perry there acting an important part. The Niagara frontier now being free from the enemy, five small vessels (the *Caledonia*, the small brig captured at Fort Erie, three schooners named the *Somers*, *Tigress*, and *Ohio*, that had been purchased, and a sloop, the *Trippe*) were thus liberated from service on the upper Niagara River, and were taken by Perry to his rendezvous at Erie, barely evading on the way the British squadron that was looking for them.

Many obstacles and delays attended Commander Perry's efforts; and when his boats were ready (they being, in addition to those previously named, the *Lawrence*, flagship, and *Niagara*, both twenty-gun brigs, and the schooners *Scorpion*, *Porcupine*, and *Ariel*, which was clipper-modelled) there were only men enough at hand to officer and man one of the brigs, despite the Commander's importunities for men sufficient to enable him to proceed against the enemy. While in this predicament Perry was annoyed—almost taunted—by letters from the Naval Department and from General Harrison, urging him to proceed against the enemy; also by the British squadron remaining in sight of his Erie harbor, threatening to attack him. A few men came straggling in, "a motley set, blacks, soldiers, and boys," and there was much sickness among them.

The second movement of the British against Fort Meigs, described on preceding pages, occurred at this time, and the British vessels moved from the offing to the west end of Lake Erie in support of it.

Master-Commander Perry's force increased, by volunteers of frontiersmen and soldiers, until at the close of July it numbered about three hundred. On August 1st, it was decided to get his ten vessels from Erie harbor into the Lake, but, owing to the shallow water on the bar, five days elapsed before his largest vessels, when empty, were floated across by great efforts, and buoying with "camels."[1]

Immediately after the vessels were in deep water, with their armament and stores placed, some of the British vessels appeared to the westward on their return. The *Ariel* and *Scorpion*

---

[1] Large scows filled with water and placed one on each side of the vessel. Upright timbers from the scows support horizontal ones through, and against, the upper parts of the forward and after portholes of the vessel, then the water is pumped from the scows to buoy the vessel.

were sent forward, and, upon their exchanging a few shots, the British Captain, Robert H. Barclay, turned his vessels around and retreated to Amherstburg.

The sailing and manœuvering qualities of Perry's squadron were then tried, and the mixed crews of amateur, inexperienced seamen were given some much-needed practice and discipline. On August 9th, Captain Jesse D. Elliott joined Commander Perry at Erie, with about one hundred officers and men of some experience, and he was given command of the *Niagara*.

The squadron left Erie on the 12th of August, 1813, and sailed toward the western part of Lake Erie. On the 15th, anchors were cast in a pleasant island harbor, that was soon to be christened by this naval force as Put-in-Bay, and have an honored record in American history.

Communications with General Harrison had been continued, and on the 16th of August Perry sailed toward the south shore, and, when off the mouth of Portage River on the 17th, he fired the signal guns agreed upon as notice to the General of his approach. Direct communications were established; and on the 19th, Generals Harrison, Cass, and McArthur, escorted by a company from the 28th Regiment United States Infantry, under

Colonel Owings (Owens?) of Kentucky, and Johnson's regiment of cavalry, together with all the seamen that could readily be found among the troops, and twenty landsmen volunteers, under Lieutenant Coburn of Payne's company, started to visit Perry on board the flagship *Lawrence.* These mixed crews were the best that could be secured to bring the number near to that necessary to man the different vessels.

They sailed on the 20th, to Put-in-Bay, to examine the island as a prospective station for the army in its advance against Amherstburg and Fort Malden.

Commander Perry kept under observation the British vessels, now all in the Detroit River, but unfavorable winds and much disability among his men, many of whom were prostrated with remittent fever, which serious disease he was also experiencing, prevented his attacking them. On the 31st, Harrison reinforced the naval squadron with thirty-six more men. On September 1st, Perry again moved to a point within sight of the enemy's squadron, but it was arranged under cover of the strong shore batteries, and would not answer his challenge.

The British had been building at Amherstburg a vessel, the *Detroit*, larger than any of those under Perry's command. At the time of her completion, provisions had become scarce at Amherstburg, and, on Friday the 10th of September, the British squadron was obliged to move eastward for supplies. The vessels were early sighted by the Americans, who decided to give battle, and prepared accordingly. Perry hoisted on his flagship, the *Lawrence*, his battle-flag bearing the dying command of Captain Lawrence in the contest of the *Chesapeake* with the *Shannon*, "*Don't Give up the Ship.*"

The battle was begun by a long-range gun of the *Detroit*, the missile falling short of its mark. Perry reserved his fire for short range. His flagship was the target for most of the enemy's shot, and the results to the brig and crew were widespread and direful. All of her guns became dismounted or useless, and only fourteen unhurt men remained, and only nine of these were seamen. The room below, to which the wounded had been taken, was above the water line and the enemy's shot frequently passed through it, continuing the work of destruction of life as well as of vessel.

Being unable to do more in the *Lawrence*, Perry ordered a boat lowered while putting on his full uniform, and, giving the *Lawrence* in charge of

Lieutenant Yarnell, with discretionary powers, he, with his small brother and four oarsmen, entered the boat and passed to the *Niagara*. He persisted in standing most of the fifteen minutes required to make the transit, and was the target of many British guns, large and small.

Taking command of the *Niagara*, Perry sent Lieutenant Elliott in a small boat to bring into close action the more distant vessels, and, raising the Commodore pennant, he changed the course of his present flagship and broke through the British line, pouring at short range, with disastrous effect, the full force of the guns right and left into the disconcerted enemy. The other American vessels followed their leader, and, in eight minutes after the *Niagara* passed through the line, the four principal British vessels surrendered. The other two, the *Chippewa* and *Little Belt*, attempted to escape, but the *Scorpion* and *Trippe*, giving chase, soon brought them back to American possession.

Lieutenant Yarnell lowered the colors of the *Lawrence* soon after the departure of Perry, and the fire of the British was thereafter directed elsewhere. They were too busy in protecting themselves, however, to take charge of the wreck.

Immediately after the surrender of the British, were written with a firm hand those model despatches which have been familiar to all students of history; the first to General William H. Harrison, viz.:

"SIR: We have met the enemy and they are ours: Two Ships, two Brigs, one Schooner, and one Sloop.
"Yours with great respect and esteem,
"O. H. PERRY."

"U. S. BRIG *Niagara*, OFF THE WESTERN SISTER [ISLAND]
"Head of Lake Erie, September 10, 1813, 4 P.M.
"SIR:
"It has pleased the Almighty to give to the arms of the United States a signal victory over their enemies on this lake. The British squadron, consisting of two ships, two brigs, one schooner, and one sloop, have this moment surrendered to the force under my command after a sharp conflict.
"I have the honor to be, sir, very respectfully,
"Your obedient servant,
"O. H. PERRY.
"Honorable WILLIAM JONES,
"*Secretary of the Navy.*"

Commander Perry decided to receive the formal surrender of the British officers on board the disabled *Lawrence*, which he did, they wending their way between the dead Americans whose bodies yet remained on the deck. The British commander, Captain Barclay, was wounded and unable to be present.

At twilight, the non-commissioned dead, of friend and foe, enveloped in shrouds, with cannon balls at their feet, were dropped one by one into the lake, after the reading of the burial service of the Episcopal Church. This sad service being completed, the vessels slowly made their way to that beautiful bay which has since been known as Put-in-Bay; and the dead officers were buried on the land which received the name Put-in-Bay Island. The losses were: American, twenty-seven killed and ninety-six wounded, of whom twenty-two killed and sixty-one wounded were aboard the *Lawrence;* British, forty-one killed and ninety-four wounded.

There are varying reports regarding the relative strength of the contending squadrons. The British had six vessels carrying sixty-three carriage guns, one on pivot, two swivels, and four howitzers. The Americans had nine vessels with fifty-four carriage guns and two swivels. The British squadron had thirty-five long guns and the American fifteen, which explains the advantage of the former in the early part of the action. In close action the weight of metal was favorable to the Americans. The British crews possessed far more naval experience than the American.[1]

This capture of the entire British squadron on these waters, the first instance in the history of America's brilliant successes on the water, had a very depressing effect on the British and their savage allies, and correspondingly opposite effect upon all three of the American armies (Northwestern, Central, and Eastern), and upon the entire populace as well. This was the continued work of young officers, Perry being but twenty-seven years of age, and his subordinates much younger.

Perry was immediately promoted to a Captaincy, and Congress gave him a vote of thanks and a medal.

---

[1] AMERICAN SQUADRON, MASTER–COMMANDER OLIVER HAZARD PERRY

Name of Vessel	Rigging	Tons Register	Total Crew	Crew Fit for Duty	Broadside, Pounds	Armament
Lawrence	Brig	480	136	105	300	2 Long 12s, 18 Short 32s.
Niagara	Brig	480	155	127	300	2 Long 12s, 18 Short 32s.
Caledonia	Brig	180	53		80	2 Long 24s, 1 Short 32.
Ariel	Schooner	112	36		48	4 Long 12s, (1 burst early).
Scorpion	Schooner	86	35		64	1 Long 32, 1 Short 32.
Somers	Schooner	94	30	184	56	1 Long 24, 1 Short 32, 2 Swivels.
Porcupine	Schooner	83	25		32	1 Long 32.
Tigress	Schooner	96	27		32	1 Long 32.
Trippe	Sloop	60	35		24	1 Long 24.
9 Vessels		1,671	532	416	936	54 Guns, 2 Swivels.

The schooner *Ohio* had gone to Erie for supplies.

Captain (acting Commodore) Barclay, in his report to the British government, expressed high praise of Commander Perry for his thoughtful and kind attention to the wounded and the prisoners, and for his magnanimity. He not only declined to take the swords from the surrendering officers, but he loaned them one thousand dollars to be expended for their comfort.

The prisoners who were able to travel were taken to Pittsburg by way of the Sanduskys and Franklinton. The wounded and sick were taken

BRITISH SQUADRON, CAPTAIN-COMMANDER ROBERT HERIOT BARCLAY

Name of Vessel	Rigging	Tons Register	Crew	Broadside, Pounds	Armament
Detroit	Ship	490	150	138	1 Long 18, 2 Long 24s, 6 Long 12s, 1 Short 18, 1 Short 24, 8 Long 9s, 1 Gun on Pivot, 2 Howitzers.
Queen Charlotte	Ship	400	126	189	1 Long 12, 2 Long 9s, 14 Short 24s, and 1 Howitzer.
Hunter	Brig	180	45	30	4 Long 6s, 2 Long 4s, 2 Long 2s, 2 Short 12s.
Lady Prevost	Brig	230	86	75	1 Long 9, 2 Long 6s, 10 Short 12s. and 1 Howitzer.
Chippewa	Schooner	70	15	9	1 Long 9, and 2 Swivels.
Little Belt	Sloop	90	18	18	1 Long 12, and 2 Long 6s.
6 Vessels		1,460	440	459	64 Guns, 4 Howitzers, 2 Swivels

Compare *Official Letters of the Military and Naval Officers of the United States during the War with Great Britain in the Years 1812, 1813, 1814, and 1815*, by John Brannan, Washington, 1823, page 207; Lossing's *War of 1812*, page 520; and *The Naval War of 1812* by Theodore Roosevelt, vol. i., pages 311, 312.

to Erie in the hospital vessels, the *Detroit*, *Queen Charlotte*, and *Niagara*. It not being practicable to repair the two first named vessels, they were left in Little Bay, Erie harbor, where they finally went to the bottom, followed a few years later by the *Niagara* which had meantime been doing good service as a receiving ship.

CHAPTER XXIV

THE AMERICANS SEEK THE BRITISH AT FORT MALDEN

Definite Preparations for the Invasion of Canada—Observance of the Day of Fasting and Prayer A Sham Battle —Enthusiastic Enlisting in Kentucky for the Invasion— Aged Aborigine Warriors Join the Ranks—The Crossing of Lake Erie—Arrival at Fort Malden—Found Deserted and Fired by the Enemy.

COLONEL RICHARD M. JOHNSON'S regiment of mounted infantry being recalled from the southwest, where it had been inadvertently sent by the Secretary of War, was ordered to escort the army supplies down the St. Marys, Auglaize, and Maumee rivers, from Forts Barbee, Amanda, and Winchester. During its sojourn in Kentucky this regiment had been recruited to over full numbers, and, by the aid of Lieutenant-Colonel James Johnson, brother of the Colonel, the discipline was brought to a high state.

About the 1st of September, with a train of

thirty wagons, and a brigade of packhorses, they started northward and arrived at Fort Winchester on the 9th, the day appointed by President Madison for fasting, humiliation, and prayer, according to Act of Congress. Captain Robert B. M'Afee, who was present, writes in his little book on the war, that:

"Those who chose to observe the day in that manner were encouraged to do so; and although there is in general but little religion to be found in the army, yet in the evening of this day a number of little parties were seen in different parts of the lines paying their devotions to the God of armies, and chanting His praises with plainness, sincerity, and zeal; whilst their less pious but moral and orderly compatriots preserved around them the strictest order and decorum. A pleasing tranquillity pervaded the ranks, and the patriot soldier seemed to feel a cheering confidence that the God of battles would shield him in the hour of danger."

Before continuing the march, a spirited and valuable disciplinary sham battle was fought in the vicinity of Fort Winchester, between the infantry and cavalry, in which the horses participated with but little less zest than their riders; and they were thus taught not to fear the noise and smoke of the guns of the infantry as their riders directed the rapid charge between their ranks.

General Harrison had invited the venerable Governor Isaac Shelby, the Revolutionary hero of King's Mountain, South Carolina, in 1781, to accompany his Kentucky troops to the invasion of Canada; and this invitation was accepted. Announcement that the Governor would be present on the march, and in the field, caused great enthusiasm in Kentucky, and nearly double the number of volunteers called for responded; thus giving General Shelby the proud command of about three thousand mounted men, exclusive of Colonel Johnson's regiment. The United States Arsenal at Newport was emptied of arms, and many of these troops were supplied at the Sanduskys, they coming through Ohio along the course of the right wing of the Northwestern Army.

Upon the arrival of General Shelby and staff at Fort Ball, they learned of Perry's victory. A despatch was at once sent to Major-General Henry, in command of the advancing reinforcements at Upper Sandusky, to hasten forward the troops. Shelby met Harrison at Fort Seneca, and, passing onward, they arrived on the 14th of September at the mouth of the Portage River, the site of the present Port Clinton, Ohio; and during the next two days the troops arrived.

General McArthur, with his force, was ordered to take command of Fort Meigs, and to deliver orders to General Clay, there in command, to move his troops to the mouth of the Portage River, where the advancing Kentuckians were to gather. McArthur was also ordered to embark artillery and provisions from Fort Meigs (which would then be reduced to the principal blockhouses in the southwest corner of the enclosure) to join the consolidating army on the Lake; and to carry orders to Colonel Johnson to go along the left bank of the Maumee River, Bay, and Lake Erie, keeping abreast of the boats. Thus all of the Northwestern Army that could be spared from garrison and guard duty was mobilized and concentrated.

The army also now embraced two hundred and sixty aged Aborigine warriors of the Wyandot, Shawnee, and Seneca tribes which Harrison had been placating. As a result of the efforts of the British to get these tribes also as allies, and of the desire of the Aborigines to be engaged in the strife, the United States government decided to enlist all who would come into its service, but with the injunction and full understanding on their part, that they must conform to the modes of civilized warfare. Harrison instructed and enjoined them that they must not kill, or injure, defenceless prisoners, old men, women, or children; and, if those fighting with him would forbear such conduct it would prove that the British could also restrain the Aborigines with them if they desired so to do. He greatly pleased them by humorously telling them that, inasmuch as he had been informed that General Proctor had promised to deliver him (General Harrison) into the hands of Tecumseh if he succeeded in capturing Fort Meigs, to be treated as that warrior might desire, he would promise to let them have Proctor as their prisoner, if they could take him, provided they would only put petticoats on him and treat him as a squaw.

These Aborigines accompanied the American army into Canada, and, presumably, were present at the Battle of the Thames, but no savage act has been imputed to them, nor to those who were subsequently subject to American command. This has been taken as additional evidence, that, if the British officers did not directly instigate, they at least willingly permitted, the massacres of prisoners who had surrendered, not to the Savages but to themselves; this, too, after their promise of protection. And they are held responsible for such acts.[1]

[1] See *History of the War of 1812*, page 303, by R. B. M'Afee, an active participant.

General Harrison was much in the saddle, personally attending to delinquents, and to business of a general nature. On September 22d, he addressed a note from Franklinton to Governor Meigs, in part as follows:

"Be pleased to send a company of one hundred men to Fort Meigs. Thirty or forty will do for Lower Sandusky. I am informed that the term of enlistment of the garrison at Fort Findlay will expire on the 22d instant. Will you be pleased to order there twenty or thirty men? . . ."

The army commenced to embark for the advance, at the mouth of Portage River, on September 20th. The vessels under command of Captain Perry were used as transports, excepting the wrecks *Lawrence*, *Detroit*, and *Queen Charlotte*, which contained the wounded, and sick, they now being airy and good hospitals. All of these vessels were viewed with great interest by the soldiers, many of whom from the interior country had never before seen such broad water and such large boats; and the many marks they bore of the fierce battle were associated with the thoughts of the complete victory of American arms they represented, to the enthusiasm of the soldiers who grew impatient for an opportunity to show their prowess in battle for their country's honor.

All the horses, even those of the officers, were left on the mainland.

It required four days to transport, by the slow-moving sail vessels, the army of nearly five thousand men, with armament and supplies, to Put-in-Bay Island. On the 25th, encampment was made on Middle Sister Island which, being but about six acres in size, afforded only close quarters.

Harrison, in company with Perry on the *Ariel*, reconnoitred the enemy at Fort Malden and at Amherstburg, and returned in time to issue a General Order to embark against them the next morning. This Order contained the following request:

"The General entreats his brave troops to remember that they are sons of sires [soldiers of the Revolutionary War] whose fame is immortal; that they are to fight for the rights of their insulted country, whilst their opponents combat for the unjust pretensions of a master. Kentuckians, remember the River Raisin, but remember it only whilst the victory is suspended. The revenge of a soldier cannot be gratified upon a fallen foe.

"By command, ROBERT BUTLER,
"*Acting Adjutant-General*." [1]

[1] The sad massacre of Kentuckians at the River Raisin nine months previous to this date by the savage allies of

The weather continued favorable, and, after seven hours' sailing, in sixteen armed vessels and nearly one hundred smaller boats, the army landed about four o'clock in the afternoon, September 27, 1813, on the sandy shore of Canada, about three miles below Amherstburg and the ill-famed Fort Malden.

There was no enemy found to dispute the land-

---

the British had, like most stirring events in war, been commemorated in song. A stanza of one of the songs often heard around the camp-fires of the Northwestern Army, runs as follows:

> "Freemen! no longer bear such slaughters;
> Avenge your country's cruel woe;
> Arouse, and save your wives and daughters!
> Arouse and smite the faithless foe!
>
> CHORUS:
> "Scalps are bought at stated prices,
> Malden pays the price in gold."

The British policy toward the Colonies, and also toward the United States, had been, as expressed in the *New Quarterly Review and British Colonial Register*, No. 4, London, following Perry's victory, as follows, viz.: ". . . We dare assert, and recent events have gone far in establishing the truth of the proposition, that the Canadas cannot be effectually and durably defended without the friendship of the Indians and command of the lakes and the River St. Lawrence. . . . We must consider the interest of the Indians as our own; for men whose very name is so formidable to an American, and whose friendship has recently been shown [in the Savage massacres of Winchester's and Dudley's troops surrendered to the British] to be of such great importance to us, we cannot do too much. . . ."

ing, or the entrance into the town. The British troops and their savage allies had hastily departed, after setting fire to the army and navy buildings, and to all the public stores they could not carry away. A detachment of troops was hurried forward, and they prevented the destruction of bridges. Upon inquiring among the few people left in the town for horses on which to mount the general officers, it was ascertained that Proctor had taken them all, more than one thousand in number; but one small pony was found and taken for General Shelby's use.

CHAPTER XXV

THE BRITISH PURSUED, AND CAPTURED AT THE THAMES

Pursuit of the British through Canada—Detroit Recovered by Americans, who Hasten to Complete Victory at the Thames—Aborigines Desert their Allies and Flock to the Americans—General Cass Appointed Military and Civil Governor of Michigan Territory—Name of Detroit's Fort Changed to that of Shelby—Kentucky Troops Return Home by Way of the Raisin.

LEAVING Colonel Smith's regiment of riflemen at Amherstburg, to guard the small boats left behind, and to guard the town from prowling Savages, the Americans pressed forward the next morning; and soon after midday they arrived at Sandwich. Captain Perry's squadron arrived in the river opposite, about the same time as did the troops.

General McArthur, with seven hundred men, was sent across the river to Detroit, to guard against the large number of Savages reported in the woods near by; and they drove away a band of Savages from the town, and found that Detroit's Fort Lernoult had been abandoned, and partly burned; and that the fire had been extinguished by the citizens who now generally welcomed the Americans.

A few days later, the Aborigines who had become discouraged by the British disasters, and did not follow Proctor's retreating columns—the Ottawas, Chippewas, Pottawotamis, Miamis, and Kickapoos—came to McArthur for peace and he reported that he had agreed with them that hostilities should cease for the present on their "agreeing to take hold of the same tomahawk with us, and to strike all who are or may be enemies of the United States, whether British or Indians. They are to bring in a number of their women and children and leave them as hostages whilst they accompany us to war. Some of them have already brought in their women, and are drawing rations." The Wyandots were soon added to the above mentioned tribes suing for peace; but no effort was made to marshal them against the British.

The martial law that had been enforced by the British at Detroit was now declared ended by proclamation of General Harrison, who also reproclaimed the civil government of the Territory of Michigan, which ended with the surrender of Hull in June, 1812.

Colonel Johnson's regiment arrived at Detroit, September 30th, with four pieces of light field artillery from Fort Meigs, and they were ordered across the river. A council of officers decided to continue the pursuit of the British by land rather than by water. McArthur and his brigade remained at Detroit; a brigade and one regiment were left at Sandwich, and the other part of the army, numbering about three thousand and five hundred, having obtained horses in addition to those of Johnson's regiment, started again the 2d of October on the track of the retreating British. Captain Perry took the heavy baggage and much of the supplies on some of his vessels to the mouth of the Thames River on Lake St. Clair; and he there learned, that some small vessels with the British cannon and heavy baggage had just escaped him, and passed up the river beyond where his vessels could go.

Evidently the British did not expect to be pursued beyond Sandwich as they did not destroy the bridges. The road being good, the Americans' progress was rapid. Seven deserters from the British were met, and the situation was learned from them. The next day, a small detachment of the British, which had been sent to destroy bridges, was captured.

Captain Perry received permission to accompany the army, and, leaving his boats well guarded, his force passed up the River Thames, their small cannon driving Aborigines and others away from partially destroyed bridges, which were speedily repaired for the pursuing army's use.

The Wyandot chief, Walk-in-the-Water, with sixty of his warriors reported, as deserters from the British, to Harrison, who, being intent after the main foe, told them to pass around to Detroit out of the way of the American army.

The British, being closely pressed, attempted to destroy their stores, and everything they could not well carry. Near Chatham they set fire to a house which contained near a thousand muskets. These were saved by the Americans. They burned other buildings, and three of their small boats, which contained artillery and heavy munitions, from which Harrison's army saved two 24-pounder cannon, and a good quantity of ammunition; and early in the morning of the 5th of October two of the British gunboats and several bateaux laden with supplies were captured, with more prisoners. The Thames was crossed at Arnold's Mill, partly by each cavalryman taking an infantryman behind him on his horse, and partly by means of the near-by bateaux.

Early in the afternoon of the 5th of October, American scouts reported the position of the combined enemy as near, and well chosen for defence. The Americans at once advanced and attacked them. The battle was sharp and decisive. The pervading spirit was, that there was to be no more withstanding of outraged Americans determined to rid their "Ohio Country" homes of the Savage incubi that for about forty years had been a blight to their own and their parents' happiness, and a blot for all time on civilization!

Johnson's cavalry broke the British lines by their impetuous charge, and, in less than five minutes (is the record) after the first shot, nearly the entire British force threw down their arms and surrendered. The Savages started their part well, but were, within a few minutes, unable to withstand the American rifles. Tecumseh was killed, whether by Colonel R. M. Johnson or other is not known; and no one could for long rally his followers. Proctor with a few followers attempted to escape in his carriage, but he was so closely pressed that he rushed into the forest on foot, and later, finding a horse, was sixty-five miles from the battle-field within twenty-four hours. His carriage, private papers, and many valuable military papers were captured. Among the battle-field captures were six brass cannon, three of which were captured from the British in the Revolutionary War but surrendered to them by Hull at Detroit.

The American loss in the Battle of the Thames was fifteen killed, and thirty wounded including the brave Colonel R. M. Johnson. The British loss was eighteen killed, twenty-six wounded, and six hundred prisoners including twenty-five officers. The Savages left thirty-three of their dead on the field. Further is not definitely known, but their loss must have been large from wounds and want of proper care, they, with Tecumseh, being carried from the field on their retreat.

The American army started on its return to Detroit the 7th of October. Harrison preceded at a more rapid pace, leaving Shelby in command. They arrived at Sandwich on the 10th, in a cold, driving storm. This storm injured several of Perry's vessels on their return from the Thames, and caused the loss of much of the military property captured. It also put a stop to the contemplated movement against Mackinac.

Report was soon received that the small British garrison had abandoned that post, which was probably not correct, as it was a rallying point for the northern Savages, and the northwestern fur trade which had been valuable to the British.

The report of the signal victory at the Thames was received throughout the United States with illuminations, bonfires, and patriotic addresses. General Harrison was lauded; and Congress afterwards gave him a vote of thanks, and a gold medal.

General Lewis Cass was appointed civil and military governor of the Territory of Michigan, and was directed to retain his brigade of soldiers, numbering about one thousand, to guard against the Savages, and to hold against invasion by the British. This appointment was confirmed by the United States Senate and Cass continued in this office several years, giving good service in his multiform duties.

The fort at Detroit was repaired, and the name Lernoult, which it had borne since 1778, was changed to Fort Shelby, in honor of Kentucky's distinguished Governor. Its site is yet indicated, and its name perpetuated, in Fort and Shelby streets.

The Kentucky volunteers were permitted to return home. They stopped at the River Raisin on their way home, and there buried such remains as could be found (sixty-five skeletons) of the massacred soldiers of General Winchester's army of the previous January. Their horses were found where left, at the mouth of Portage River, Ohio.

The Savages, the much valued allies of the British, were left without food for the winter after the defeat of them and their allies at the Battle of the Thames. They had been tutored to war, and to complete subserviency to the British, and had lost interest in hunting wild game for their subsistence. As at the close of the Revolutionary War, they turned at once, and with as little apparent regret for their past hostilities, to the Americans for their support. As formerly, they gathered at Detroit in such great number that they could not be fully fed by the Americans, who were, themselves, scantily supplied. They went about the streets gathering and devouring, so far as they could, whatever of fragmentary food that could be given them by the soldiers and citizens.

Harrison dealt kindly with them; and he assembled them at Greenville, Ohio, July 22, 1814, where a lasting treaty was effected for their best interest.

CHAPTER XXVI

THE OHIO COUNTRY FREE FROM THE SAVAGE ALLIANCE

Proctor's Request and Harrison's Reply—Harrison Goes to Reinforce Army of the Centre—Period of Quiet in the Ohio Country—General Harrison Resigns—Renewed Efforts for Defence and Advance—Scarcity of Food and Money—Further Neglect by Eastern Authorities—Expeditions through Canada—Unfortunate Expedition to the North.

AFTER providing for the garrisoning of the several forts in the old Northwestern Territory, General Harrison, with about thirteen hundred soldiers, sailed in Captain Perry's squadron for Buffalo[1] where they arrived the 24th of

[1] General Harrison received by messenger Lieutenant Le Breton a letter from Major-General Proctor dated October 18th (place of writing not given), addressed to him at the Moravian towns by the Thames, but delivered at Detroit before his departure from that place. This letter requested the return of private papers and property captured at the Battle of the Thames; also a request for mild treatment of the British prisoners and subjects. This writing of Proctor was considered by Harrison unnecessary,

October, 1813, to co-operate with the Army of the Centre; but Harrison did not remain there as a party to the resulting defeats.

On account of antagonisms in the War Department General Harrison's able and successful work in the War of 1812-14 had been nearly completed. He returned to his family in Cincinnati, where he retained head-quarters until he resigned from the army, his resignation to take effect May 31, 1814.

The West and Northwest experienced comparative quiet after the Battle of the Thames.

---

as such conduct had been already provided for, and, further, it was asking from him what Proctor had not been known to accord to Americans. Lieutenant Le Breton was given good opportunity to see that the proprieties of civilization had been complied with in regard to the British prisoners. He was not permitted to return by land, however, but was taken across Lake Erie in boat with Harrison.

He was given in reply a letter dated "Headquarters, Fort George, November 3, 1813," addressed, not to Proctor but to Major-General Vincent the ranking officer. This reply cited three instances, of the many in addition to Winchester's and Dudley's troops, of atrocious Savage murders and mutilations committed on inoffensive American men, women, and children by Savage members of the British army whose officers were at least privy to the deeds and did not subject their perpetrators to discipline. Eloquent protest was again made against such atrocious warfare, and demand for its cessation, adding that, "The effect of these barbarities will not be confined to the present generation. Ages to come will feel the deep rooted hatred and enmity which they must produce between the nations."

However, food and money again became scarce, and some successes of the British over the Army of the Centre again brought anxiety to this region. The difficulties of properly meeting the requirements for success in this, the then "distant western country," in all questions in which eastern authorities had the dictation, are shown (as a repetition of the old, old story) in the following extracts from a letter to Governor Meigs written by General John S. Gano dated "Headquarters Ohio Militia, Lower Sandusky, January 16, 1814," viz.:

"I have the pleasure to inform you that after repeated solicitations and much delay, the paymaster has succeeded in obtaining two months' pay for the troops under my command. I have sent him on to Detroit, as the men there are in great want of money to purchase necessaries, etc.

"Yesterday the Lieutenant and Surgeon of the Navy, Champlain and Eastman, left this post for Put-in-Bay. They arrived the evening before, and report they have everything arranged to give the enemy a warm reception should they visit them. About forty pieces of cannon can be brought to play upon them at any point. I find, however, that they want men. I shall send in the regulars from Seneca as soon as possible, to reinforce them which is absolutely necessary from the Lieutenant's representations to me. We have not had the detailed account from Buffalo, etc.

"Majors Vance and Meek have just arrived from Detroit, and give a favorable account from that quarter as to the exertions of Colonel Butler, to whom I sent Major Vance as an express. There is a detachment under Major Smiley up the River Thames who will, I hope, fare better than Larwell. The militia are very tired of the service there, and all are beginning to count days. They have had an immense deal of fatigue and severe duty to perform.

"The fort at Portage [by the Portage River, northwestern Ohio] is progressing and is the best piece of work in the Western country as to strength. The men draw the timber to admiration—eighty or ninety logs a day without a murmur. The teams have been, and are, useless for want of forage. The greatest part have actually died. I wrote in November to Quartermaster Gardiner for funds to be sent to the Quartermaster's assistant here to purchase forage, which could have been obtained two or three hundred miles from here. If three hundred dollars could have been sent on, I think it would have saved the United States three thousand; and I assure you I have used every exertion to preserve and protect the public property.

"As I before observed, nothing will induce the militia to remain after their term of service expires, which will be the last of next month. . . . I am only anxious on account of the public property that may be left exposed.

"I have this post in a tolerable state of defence, as well as all the posts I command, which, you know, are scattered from Dan to Beersheba; and each must rely on its own strength for its defence. I have had an immense detail business in communication, etc.

"Flour is very scarce at all the frontier posts. I have been between 'hawk and buzzard'—the commissary and contractor; and between the two, as is usual, must fail. What a wretched system of warfare! . . .

"P. S. An express by a naval officer has just arrived from Erie. Lieutenant Packet has given me a full account of the loss of the posts below, at Niagara. The enemy possessed themselves of the artillery, military stores, etc., etc., to a large amount; and there is no doubt but an attempt to take or destroy the vessels at Put-in-Bay will be attempted, and Captain Elliott has requested a reinforcement of two hundred men to send to the Island, which I have not the power to furnish. I have ordered a few regulars from Seneca, and will send a few militia. My troops are so scattered, I have no disposable force without evacuating some of the posts that contain considerable military stores. I wrote to General Harrison, some time since, recommending him to send on the recruits. They certainly will be wanted as soon as the British can move on the ice or by water to Detroit or the Islands. I fear we shall lose all that has been gained, unless great exertions are used to reinforce; and supply of provisions is much wanted."

The garrison of Fort Meigs had suffered much from short rations, and, about the middle of January, some of the soldiers of the garrison were sent up the river to Fort Winchester where they obtained as much food as they could carry; and

From 1813-1814

they transported it to Fort Meigs as best they could. Eighty soldiers, a large part of this garrison, were reported sick January 27, 1814.

The fears of attack by the enemy, expressed by General Gano, were not realized; but fears were often excited during the summer and fall.

Lieutenant-Colonel Butler, in temporary command at Detroit, being informed during the last of January or early in February, that a body of British, Canadians, and Savages, were by the River Thames near Chatham, sent Captain Lee, with a squad of cavalry, to investigate. They went around the enemy, attacked them fiercely, scattered them, taking several prisoners, including Colonel Babie (Bahbie) who led a collection of western Savages to the New York frontier the summer or fall of 1813.

A little later in February, 1814, Lieutenant-Colonel Butler sent one hundred and sixty soldiers, with two six-pounder cannon, under Captain Jeremiah Holmes, against the British Fort Talbot, one hundred miles or more from Detroit, on the north shore of Lake Erie. Deeming it unwise to attack the fort with his small force, Captain Holmes passed across the country to Delaware on the Thames, where the enemy, superior in numbers, led him on to the Longwoods where they gave battle for an hour about dark on March 3d. Both parties withdrew during the night. The American loss was seven killed and wounded. These incursions, while showing great activity of the Americans in keeping the enemy busy in his own domain, lost much of their design from the necessarily small forces employed.

Early in July, 1814, a small squadron of vessels was sent out from Detroit for the capture of Fort Mackinac and other points in that region important to the British fur trade. Some time had been given to preparation for this expedition. Arthur St. Clair was in command of the vessels *Niagara*, *Caledonia*, *Scorpion*, *St. Lawrence*, and *Tigress;* and George Croghan, now a Lieutenant-Colonel, was in command of the five hundred United States troops, and two hundred and fifty militia, which had quarters on the vessels. When the squadron arrived at Fort Gratiot, recently built by order of General McArthur at the head of St. Clair River (Strait), Croghan's force was augmented by Colonel William Colgreave's regiment of Ohio volunteers, and Captain Gratiot. A desired attack on a new British post by Matchadach Bay was abandoned, after a several days' trial to get through the narrow channels between the islands, in foggy weather and without a proper pilot. Sailing to Fort St. Joseph, toward Lake Superior, they found it abandoned. The buildings here were destroyed by part of the expedition, while others pressed forward to the Sault Ste. Marie, where they arrived July 21st, to find that John Johnson, "a renegade magistrate from Michigan," agent of the British Northwest Company, had just departed with his assistants, carrying away all the property possible, and setting fire to the company's sloop. This fire was extinguished by the Americans, but the vessel proving unseaworthy, she was again fired. After destroying the buildings, the Americans returned to St. Joseph, and the reunited forces arrived at Mackinac July 26th.

Deciding that it was unwise for the vessels to attack the fort, Croghan's men were landed, and proceeded to a rear attack. They were met by such severe fire by the British and concealed Savages, that they retreated to the boats with a loss of thirteen killed, including Major Holmes, and fifty-five wounded, including Captains Van Horn and Desha, and Lieutenant Jackson. Two were missing.

Passing to the Nautawassaga River, they captured the blockhouse three miles from its mouth, but the valuable furs of the Northwest

Company had been taken away, and their vessel burned.

The expedition now sailed for Detroit, leaving the *Tigress*, with Captain Champlain, and the *Scorpion*, with Captain Turner, and crews of nearly thirty men each, as blockaders to cut off supplies intended for the garrison at Mackinac. They served this purpose effectually until the night of September 3d, when the *Tigress*, being alone, was captured by a stealthy and overwhelming force of the enemy; which force also deceived the *Scorpion's* officers and crew to a close contact when she was boarded and overwhelmed.

These disasters, with the loss of the post at Prairie du Chien, west of Lake Michigan, on July 17th, again increased the apprehensions of the Americans throughout the Northwest.

The Savages becoming more aggressive around Lake Michigan, General McArthur was directed to gather mounted men to proceed against them. He arrived at Detroit, from Ohio, on October 9th, with about seven hundred men, gathered from Ohio and Kentucky. At this time, the American army, under General Jacob Brown, was being sorely pressed on the Niagara frontier, and McArthur decided to divert some of the British forces from that point; and he executed the most daring expedition of the war through Canada. Starting northward from Detroit, after the middle of October, with seven hundred and fifty men and five small field cannon, he circled around Lake St. Clair, crossed the River St. Clair on the 26th, moved rapidly through the Scotch settlement of Baldoon, the Moravian towns by the Thames, and London, arriving at Oxford, November 4th. Here he found a considerable force of militia, which he disarmed and paroled; and he punished those who violently opposed him by burning their houses. He moved eastward, and passed through Burford to Brantford, by the Grand River. Here, being opposed by the Iroquois Aborigines resident there, also by the British and militia, he turned southward, attacked the militia at Malcolm Hill, by the Grand River, killing and wounding seven and taking one hundred and thirty-one prisoners. The only American loss on this expedition was one killed and six wounded in the last engagement. The flouring mill and its belongings here were destroyed; also several mills on his way to Dover by Lake Erie. These mills had been the chief source of supply to the British in their operations against the Army of the Centre. At Dover, McArthur turned westward, passed through Simcoe, St. Thomas, and near the Thames, being pursued some distance by eleven hundred British regulars. On the 17th of November this brilliant and successful expedition ended at Sandwich. Meantime the western Aborigines went into winter quarters, and all of the volunteers in McArthur's command, who so desired, were discharged.

General McArthur returned to Ohio, and, with his superiors, discussed ways and means for a yet more active work against the enemy.

Overtures for peace having been made, however, and peace commissioners appointed by Great Britain and the United States, a treaty closing the war was signed at Ghent, Belgium, December 24, 1814; and then came the time when the United States first entered into the full, peaceable, continued possession and jurisdiction of the territory west of the Allegheny Mountains, and of all its people, of which and whom they had been mainly deprived for thirty years after the Revolutionary War, notwithstanding the Treaty of Paris.

CHAPTER XXVII

SUCCESS OF THE WAR FOR INDEPENDENCE ASSURED

The Treaty of Ghent Closing the War of 1812-14—Further Confirmation of American Claim of Notorious Methods.

THE Treaty of Ghent was not completed without difficulty. What were considered by Americans as unjust and extortionate claims by Great Britain, were urged by her Commissioners for recognition, and are here presented as further confirmation of the truth of the direct assertions and characterizations on preceding pages of her wicked policy with the American Aborigines, and toward Americans, before, during, and between the wars of these countries with each other.

President Madison's Messages to Congress during the last war, from May 25, 1813; the discussions of Congress; other American State Papers during the war; and the contentions of the Commissioners of both parties, were considered by Americans as quite sufficient answer to Great Britain's Declaration relative to the War of 1812, issued from Westminster January 9, 1813.

The Peace Commissioners for the War of 1812-14—Lord Gambier, Henry Goulburn, and William Adams on the part of Great Britain, and John Quincy Adams, James A. Bayard, Henry Clay, Jonathan Russell, and Albert Gallatin on the part of the United States—met in Ghent, Belgium, August 6, 1814, and did not agree upon the form of the treaty until December 24th.

For a long time the wide differences of claims portended permanent disagreement; but gradually, after conferences with the respective home governmental authorities, recession from one objectionable point after another was made by each party, the British yielding their most obnoxious claims, until the treaty, as signed, was not fully satisfactory to either country.

The principal complaints of the United States against Great Britain, causing the War of 1812, were the search of her vessels, the impressment of her seamen, the blockade of her ports, and the domination of the Western Aborigines. The first named points were not gained in the treaty, which caused great regret in the East particularly, though their modification was promised. The British felt no need later for the blockade. Some indefinite boundaries in the East, and between Lake Superior and the Mississippi River, were adjusted.

Early in the treaty negotiations, the British Commissioners quibbled against the American claims regarding their conduct with the Aborigines. They boldly, and persistently, claimed them as "their allies," and wanted recognition of them as such! They held that the United States should set apart much of the Ohio Country for their especial use; that the United States' treaties with them were like treaties between individual nations; that "the American Government now for the first time, in effect, declared that all Indian nations within its Line of Demarkation are its Subjects, living there upon sufferance, on Lands which it also claims the exclusive right of acquiring [*sic*], thereby menacing the final extinction of these Nations," to which they formally protested, and stated that their instructions on this subject were peremptory.

The American Commissioners replied pointedly, and asked what meant all of the old English charters, from that of Virginia by Queen Elizabeth, to that of Georgia by the immediate predecessor of King George III., if the Aborigines were the sovereigns and proprietors of the lands bestowed by those charters?

The British continued their endeavors, however, to make all negotiations hinge on their question regarding the Aborigines, "their allies whom they must protect." The Americans positively objected to including the Aborigines in the treaty as "Allies of Great Britain," which would indicate that they were British subjects; and this objection prevailed after long diplomatic struggle.

The continued inebriation of successive generations of American Aborigines, and their education and confirmation in savagery, for thirty years after the Treaty of Paris, as before, forced upon the United States not only an untold amount of savagery, suffering, and loss of life among her citizens, but later left an evil heritage, of enormous proportions, of evil and degenerate habits of the Aborigines, from which the American nation has not yet fully recovered, notwithstanding the expenditure of money and efforts for their control, and civilization, many times in excess of such expenditures by any other nation for barbarous and savage people.

However, it may well be written that the forbearance of offence, the magnanimity toward the conquered, the efforts, money, and lives expended by Americans to secure their freedom, and some of their rights, have borne much wholesome fruit, and thought, for the tempering of the savage barbarity of nations; and thereby this great forbearance, suffering, and magnanimity have already been a blessing to humanity at large, that will be more fully recognized and appreciated in the future than it has been in the past.

Throughout the long months of diplomatic struggle at Ghent, the American Commissioners maintained a commendable patience, composure with alertness, and wisdom, which won their contention regarding the Aborigines, the honor of the western country, and of the nation, on this most important question.

The questions of search and impressment of seamen could not long remain without honorable settlement, after proper diplomatic relations between the two countries were established.

The signing of the Treaty of Ghent obscured the last hope of designing nations for the possession of the Ohio Country. All of this vast and invaluable region was again, and fully, saved to the American Union.

This War of 1812-1814 also produced a condition of wholesome national unity, and a forbearing regard for the Union throughout the East and the West, that was unknown before.

It appears befitting that a few words be added regarding the later history of the Aborigines who chose to remain in the United States.

The British continued to trade with those along the borders, and kept alive their thirst for spirituous liquors, as did many United States traders, clandestinely. As late as July, 1832, the British traders attracted to Fort Malden, Amherstburg, Canada, one of the largest gatherings of Aborigines of record. They were gathered from most parts of the United States, embracing even the Flatheads of the extreme West. This meeting, and the great flow of intoxicants, spoiled the work of the American religious missionaries at the nearby station. There was, however, little, if any, successful effort of the British agents after the Treaty of Ghent to federate the Aborigines for war against the United States.

This government continued the policy of enforcing temperance among these wards of the nation; also the policy of treating with them and purchasing their claims to lands not needed by them for agricultural purposes, but needed by citizen settlers; in consonance with the truism that no barbarous people, and much less savage ones, have right to lands for hunting purposes, that are needed for civilized people and for the advance of civilization.

Nearly all of these Aborigines were removed west of the Mississippi River in the 1830's and early 1840's.

Schools founded by the United States, as well as denominational religious schools, have multiplied for their education by means of book and industrial methods. Many have become citizens, and own land in severalty. Through the paternal methods of the general government, many are now wealthy and prospering.

INDEX

A

Aborigines, condition of, 3-15; after Revolutionary War, 19; after Treaty of Greenville, 162; aggressors, 52-53; American captives with, 38; forbidden to buy land from, 22; efforts for best interest of, 202, 306-309; inquiries regarding, 46, 48-50, 82; lesson to, against British savagery, 279; short rations to, at Detroit, 291; treaties with, *see under* Treaties; British allowances to, 20, 184-185, 189; Dorchester's speech to, 100; keep them hostile to Americans, 45, 50, 104, 107, 183-190; incite them to savagery, 6, 11, 60, 80, 83-85; inebriate them, 11, 14, 177, 308; fight with them against Americans, 12, 103, 107, 114-116, 225-228, 239-242, 254-255, 257, 282, 288; alliance with them the most inhuman in history, 26; dread of, 8; desire to federate them against Americans, 6, 8, 84, 90, 98, 100; forsaken by them, 242, 285, 287; gain from fur trade with, 4, 80, 182; govern and guard them, 50, 100, 261; short rations to, 20-22, 118; supply them with weapons, 11, 85, 178, 185, 189; cannibalism of, 50, 77, 193, 202, 227, 240; celebrate victories with British, 12-15, 60; chiefs of, 78-79, 142-143, 226, 287; cloyed by warrings of British and French, 7; councils, great, by Maumee, 83, 90; drawn to peace by Gen. Wayne, 133-136; friendship of few aged, to Americans, 244, 250, 260, 278-279; lesson in American patriotism, 139; new generation of, 175; payments by U. S. to, 47, 164, 169, 178-179; peace with U. S. they did not want, 78; begged for, 285; efforts of U. S. for, 80, 82-83, 86, 111; Prophet, the, 174; reservations for, 170-171; tribes at great councils, 84, 90; at the greatest treaty with, 141; savagery of the, 47, 52-53, 77, 82, 250

Adair, Major John, 85
Adams, John, 25, 27, 155
Adams, Colonel, 209
Allen, Col. John, 207, 224
American grievances, and claims, against Great Britain, 91, 92; military posts in 1809-12, 175-189; *Pioneer* magazine quoted, 77
Amherstburg, Canada, 147
Anderson, Colonel, 248
Armed vessels on Lake Erie: American, 272; British, 273
Armies, American: Harmar's, 54-58; Harrison's, 190, 206-212, 228-293; Hull's,

Index

Armies—*Continued*
196, 199; surrender of, 202;
St. Clair's, 66–77; Wayne's,
86, 95, 108–124; Winchester's, 212–227; against
France and Spain, 155
Armstrong, John, Judge, 44
Arnold, Benedict, at Detroit,
44
Ashton, Captain, 66
Atherton, William, book on
N. W. Army, 219
Atwater, Caleb, *History of
Ohio*, 76

B

Ball, Colonel, 252
Banner, British surgeon, 260
Barbee, Colonel Joshua, 213
Battles: of Fallen Timber,
113, 126; of Harmar's
army at head of Maumee
River, 56–58; of St. Clair's
army at head of Wabash,
68; Winchester's at the
Raisin, 227; sham, for
discipline, 276; of the
Thames, Canada, 288; of
Tippecanoe, 190; naval,
on Lake Erie, 268–269;
siege of Ft. Meigs, 235–239
Black Rock, N. Y., 262–263
Bond, Phineas, Am. Consul,
28
Bondie, Antoine, 210
Boyd, Ensign, 96
Brant, Capt. Joseph (Br.),
42, 63, 87
Brickell, John, captive, 137–138
British, advance and retreat of, 213–214; advantages of, 93, 128–129; all of
naval force of, on Lake Erie
captured, 269; Am. efforts
to learn methods of, with
Savages, 83; animus of, 23–26; 27–32, 41–44, 50, 60, 63,
90, 94, 99, 100–101, etc.;
army captured at the
Thames, 288; build Ft.
Malden, 147, and abandon
it to Americans, 283; capture Hull's baggage, 200;
conspire against American
Union, 41, 173–193; efforts
for alliance with Savages,
6, 8, 11–15, 20, 42, 90, 100,
168, 244, etc.; embarrassment of, with Aborigines,
21; fight with Savages
against Americans, 11–15,
103, 114, 116, 235, 239,
288; flee before Americans,
283; governed by commercial and ulterior interests, 23, 32, 41, 78 80,
182; hold Am. forts, 23;
strengthen them, 43, 102,
118, 128; build Forts Miami
and Turtle Island in U. S.,
101; invade U. S., 101, 159;
last claim of the Savages
as their allies, 305–306;
martial law of, superseded
by Am. civil law, 285;
obstruct Am. development
and peace, 32, 36, 63, 82,
87–91; promote savagery,
11–15, 104–107, 145, 173–
177, 183–186, 188–189;
scouts of, 234; supply
Savages with weapons
against Americans, 85, 178,
189; surrender forts in
U. S., 148
Brown, John, of Kentucky, 62
Brownstown, Michigan,
treaty at, 171, 261
Brush, Capt. Henry, saves
his command, 203
Buntin, Capt. Robert, 154
Burbeck, Major Henry, 97
Burke, Reverend, 136
Burr, Aaron, 165
Butler, Col. John (Br.), 87
Butler, Lieut.-Col., 295, 297
Butler, Richard, Treaty-Com., 35; Gen., slain, 74

Index 313

C

Campbell, Lieutenant, 241
Campbell, Maj. William (Br.), 115
Canada, preparations for invasion of, 277–278; advance of Am. army into, 280–282; expeditions through, 280–282, 295, 297–302
Cannibalism of the Savages, 50, 77, 193, 202, 227, 240
Carleton, Sir Guy, 11; see Dorchester, Lord
Carmarthen, Marquis of, 27
Cass, Lewis, Col., 199; Gen., 252; Gov. of Michigan, 290
Champlain, Lieut., 294, 300
Chatham, Lord, quoted, 25
Chauncey, Com. Isaac, 263
Chew, Joseph (Br. Sec.), 129
Chicago, 193, 201
Chickasaw Bluffs, Miss., 180
Chillicothe, Ohio, 198
Chittenden, Thomas, Gov., 24
Cincinnati, Ohio, named, 49
Civil government organized: in counties: Hamilton, 49; extended, 81; Kent, 151; Knox, 54; St. Clair, 49; Washington, 46; Wayne, 151; States: Kentucky, 85; Ohio, 162; Territories: Illinois, 172; Indiana, 158; Kentucky, 54; Louisiana, 160; Michigan, 165; Mississippi, 156; Missouri, 192; Northwestern, 44, 157; Ohio, 158
Clark, Col. George R., 14, 35, 40
Clark, Gen. William, 175–176, 184
Clarksville, Kentucky, 49
Clay, Gen. Green, 237, 245, 250, 252–253
Clinton, Gov. George, New York, 24
Colgreve, Col. William, 298

Communication, development of, 161
Connecticut cedes to the U. S. claims in Ohio, 39, 158; payments of land company to Aborigines, 164
Connolly, John, 43
Conspiracy of British and Tecumseh, 173–193; of Chief Nicholas, 6; of Pontiac, 7
Cornplanter, Seneca chief, 84
Croghan, Capt. George, 248, 257–259, 298–299
Councils, great Aborigine, 83–91

D

Danville, Kentucky, 52
Davidson, Lieutenant, 200
Dayton, Ohio, 196
Debts, individual Br., State laws regarding, 28
Defiance, Ohio, 213, 214, 216; see Fort Defiance
Denny, Ebenezer, report of St. Clair's defeat, 68, 75
De Peyster, Maj. Arent S., 14, 19, 21
Desha, Captain, wounded, 299
Detroit, principal Br. post, 10–17, 43, 45, 50, 55, 65, 87, 99–101, 114, 120; surrendered to Americans, 148–149, 151, 154; British invade, 159; treaty at, 169; trading post at, 181, 196, 198; surrendered to Br., 202; again occupied by Americans, 285; Gen. Shelby at, 290; short rations at, 291
Dickson, Scotch trader, 245
Dill, Captain, 197
Doolan, James, 253
Dorchester, Lord, engaged in savage work, 11, 43; addresses Savages, 100,

Index

Dorchester—*Continued*
102; orders surrender of Am. forts, 147
Douglas, Ephraim, Am. agent to Aborigines, 19,.22
Doughty, Major, 49
Dudley, Col. William, massacred, 238
Dunlap, Colonel, 198
Dwight, Th., preferred disunion to war, 99

E

Eastman, Surgeon, 294
Elliott, Captain, 296
Elliott, Lieut. Jesse D., 262–263, 266
Elliott, Matthew, Br. agent, Capt. and Col., 83, 88, 100, 106, 147, 214
Emissaries, British, French, and Spanish, 99, 192; Spanish, 152, 154; the Prophet's, 175
England, Col. Richard (Br.), 101, 106, 119, 146
Erie, Pa., 263, 265–266, 296
Eustis, William, 198
Expeditions, against the Savages, 38, 48, 51–52, 64, 66, 220–221; through Canada, 280–282, 295, 297–302; against Mackinac, 298–300
Explorers, French, 1; British, 2

F

Fasting and Prayer, day of, 276
Federalists, adverse influence of, 99, 161, 186–187
Findlay, Col. James, 197–198, 213
Findlay, Ohio, 198
Firelands, 164
Forts: abandoned by British in 1796, 145; Adams in Ohio, 109, 124, in Mississippi, 157; Amanda, 215; Auglaize, 125; Ball, 217; Barbee, 213, 215, 217, Dearborn, Chicago, 181; 201; Defiance, 111, 112, 114, 116, 117, 121, 122, 124–126, 137, 138; Deposit, Wayne's, 112, 113, Winchester's, 223, 228–229; Erie, British, 88, 262–263; Feree, 216; Findlay, 190, 198, 217; Finney, 37; George at Niagara, 227, 264; Greenville, 96, 105, 123, 125; Hamilton, 67, 73, 83, 85; Harmar, 46; Harrison, 210, 211, 213; Hawkins, Ga., 180; Industry, 164–165; in 1801, 160; Jefferson, 67, 76, 96, 97; Jennings, 213, 215; Lernoult, Detroit, 13, 147, 148, 290; Loramie, 125; McArthur, 197, 217; Mackinac, 147, 181, 201, 298; Madison, 181; Malden, British, 147, 168, 189, 192, 200–201, 214; Massac, 100, 252; Meigs, 230–231; besieged, 235–243, 251, 278, 297; Miami, British, 101, 102, 115, 119, 145; Miami, American, 147, 148, 201; Necessity, 197, 217; Osage, 181; Piqua, 125; Pitt, 48; Portage, 229, 252, 295; Prairie du Chien, 300; Recovery, 97, 102, 105; Refuge, 85, 187, 205; St. Clair, 96; St. Joseph, 299; St. Marys 125; St. Stephens, 180; Seneca, 251; Shelby, 290; Spanish, 153, 157; Stephenson, 256; Steuben, 48, 66; Turtle Island, British, 101, 118, 119; Vincennes, 40, 48; Washington, 49, 54, 57, 67, 95, 148; Wayne, 56, 124, 132, 135, 137, 140, 162, 178, 181, 186, 188, 193; besieged, 207–208, 210; Winchester, 216, 229, 245, 276, 296

Index

Fourth of July celebrations, 139, 249
France and Spain, offended by Jay Treaty, 152–155; emissaries of, 99, 152, 154
Frankfort, Kentucky, 205
Franklin, Benjamin, quoted about the British, 28
Fremont, Ohio, 217
Fur trade, American, 92, 163, 182; British, 4, 80, 182

G

Gaines, Colonel, 254
Gamelin, Antoine, peace agent, 49
Gano, Gen. John S., report, 294–296
Gardiner, Quartermaster, 295
Germain, Lord, savagery of, 11
Ghent, Treaty of Independence at, 302–307
Gibson, Captain, slain, 105
Girty, Simon, renegade, 88
Grasson, Surgeon, slain, 74
Gratiot, Captain, 298
Greenville, Ohio, Wayne's treaty at, 139–143; second treaty at, 291; see Fort Greenville

H

Haldimand, Sir Frederick, Gov. of Canada, 23, 24
Hamilton, Alexander, 93
Hamilton, Captain, 237
Hamilton, Henry, Lieut.-Gov. of Canada, 10
Hamilton, Ohio, 67
Hammond, George, 1st Br. Min., 31, 91, 93
Hamtramck, Maj. John F., 54, 82, 132–133; report, 145–146, 148
Hardin, Col. John, 48, 56–57, 64; murdered by Savages, 82
Harmar, Gen. Josiah, 40, 45, 51; disastrous ex. agt. Savages, 54–58, 67
Harrison, William H., Sec. N. W. Ter., 156; 1st Rep. in Cong., 157; 1st Gov. of Ind., 158, 163, 175, 177–178; Gen., 182–184, 186–187; at Battle of Tippecanoe, 190; visits Kentucky 205–207; supersedes Gen. Winchester, 214–216, 228; builds Ft. Meigs, 230, 231, 234; broad supervision of, 248, 252–253, 256; urged bldg. armed vessels on Lake Erie, 263; captures Br. army at the Thames, 288; goes to aid Army of the Centre, 292; resigns military com., 293; at second Treaty of Greenville, 291
Heald, Nathan, in com. Ft. Dearborn, Chicago, 193
Henley, Samuel, Quartermaster, 148
Hicks, Lieut. Porter, surrenders Ft. Mackinac, 201
Holmes, Capt. Jeremiah, ex. through Canada, 297; slain, 299
Hospital ships, 280
Howard, Spanish General, 153
Howard, Gov. of Missouri Territory, 192, 206
Hull, William, Col., 24; Gov. Mich. Ter., 165, 167–168, 171, 177, 185, 193; urges mil. and naval forces, 195–196; commissioned Brig.-Gen., and marches to Detroit, 196–201; surrenders to Br., 202–203
Hunt, Col. Thomas, 207

I

Illinois Country, 48, 99
Illinois Territory organized, 205

Indiana Territory organized, 205
Indians, a misnomer, 5; see Aborigines
Inefficiency of U. S. Government, 151
Inness, Judge Henry, 52, 62
Interpreters at Treaty of Greenville, 141
Ironside, George, Br. trader, advice of, to Savages, 126

J

Jackson, Lieut., wounded, 299
Jefferson, Thomas, Gov. of Va., 16; Sec. of State, 31; in Congress, 34; Sec. of State, 93; against Spanish, 100; President, for La. pur., 160; advice to savages, 167–168
Johnson, Col. Guy, Br. agent, 26, 84
Johnson, Lieut.-Col. James, 275
Johnson, Sir John, Br. agent, ad. to Savages, 22, 42, 84
Johnson, Col. John, 181, 185–186
Johnson, John, renegade, 299
Johnson, Col. Richard M., 208, 245, 248–249, 275, wounded, 289
Johnson, Stephen, clerk, slain, 211
Johnson, Sir William, Br. Supt., 84

K

Kaskaskia, Illinois, 54
Kentucky, 53; organized as Territory, 54; troops of, 54, 56, 103, 108, 123, 205–208, 240, 277; Board of War of, 62; organized as State, 85; disunion emissaries in, 99, 152
Kethtipecanunk, Ind., 65

King George III., timidity of, 25; for savagery, 26
Knox, Gen. Henry, Sec. of War, 24, 47; reports of, 75, 80–91

L

Lafayette, Ind., 64
Lake Erie, armed vessels recommended for, 196, 262–264
Lake St. Clair, 280, 289, 301
Land offices in Ohio, 158
Land titles at Vincennes, 49; in Ohio, 158
Larwell, Major, in Canada, 295
Lasselle, brothers, deserters from Br., 133–134
LeChauvre, Br. trader, 136
Lee, Arthur, Treaty Com., 35
Lee, Captain, expedition through Canada, 297
Leftwich, Va. General, 231
Le Maître, Francis, Br. Mil. Sec., 119
Lewis, Capt., messenger to Canada, 147–148
Lewis, Col. William, 207, 224, 227
Lincoln, Benjamin, Sec. of War, 19; Peace Com., 86
Loftus Heights, Miss., 157
Logan, Benjamin, on Board of War, 62
Logan, Capt. John, 207-8
Loss of life, 38, 45, 47, 51–53; in Harmar's army, 58, 64, 66; in St. Clair's army, 74, 82, 86, 96, 102–105; in Wayne's army, 114, 121–122, 187; in Harrison's army, 191, 213, 219–221; Winchester's army, 226–227; at siege of Fort Meigs, 235, 238, 242–243, 250–251; at Fort Stephenson, 257–258; in Perry's battle on Lake Erie, 271; in Harrison's battle of the Thames

Loss of life—*Continued*
289; in expeditions in Canada, and North, 298-299, 301
Lower Sandusky, Ohio, now Fremont, 217
Lowry, Lieut., slain, 96

M

M'Afee, Capt. Robert B., 208, 219, 251, 276, 279
McArthur, Col. Duncan, 196, 198; General, 252, 278, 286; exp. through Canada, 300-302
McCune, Captain, 252-253
McKee, Alexander, Br. agent, 85, 87, 91, 100, 104-106, 115, 118, 119, 127, 129, 134, 168, 185
McKeehan, Surgeon, 260-261
McMahon, Major, 102-103
McPherson, Captain, 200
Madison, Maj. George, 226-227
Madison, Pres. James, 198, 303
Marietta, Ohio, 49
Marschalk, Captain, 148
Mason, J., Supt. trading agencies, 180
Massachusetts cedes claim in the Ohio Country, 36
Massacres by the Savages, 79, 202, 221, 238, 241
Massie, Lieutenant, 134-135
May, William, 83, 85
Meek, Major, 295
Meigs, Gov. Return J., 196, 202, 205
Miami Villages, 50, 56-57, 66, 110, 122, 132
Michigan Territory organized 165; under British rule until 1796, 148; settlements in, 191-192; 285-286, 290
Miller, Christopher, captive, 111, 114
Missouri Territory organized, 192

Money, kinds of in 1796, 149
Montjoy, Lieutenant, 252
Montreal merchants lose trade, 80
Morris, Gouverneur, agent to London, 28
Morrow, Jeremiah, Peace Com., 202
Muir, Br. Major, 234, 238
Murray, Br. Major Patrick, 55

N

Navarre, Peter, messenger, 225
Navigation of Mississippi River, 39, 40, 99
Navies on Lake Erie, Am. and Br., 262-273
Newport, Kentucky, U. S. Arsenal in, 277
Niagara, 199; frontier relieved, 300-302
Northwestern Territory, conditions in 1814, 294-296. *See* under Civil Organizations

O

Ohio Company of Associates, 37
Ohio Country, efforts to open for settlers, 36; increasing interest in, 157; uniform land titles in, 49, 158
Ohio Territory, population of in 1796 and 1800, 159; in 1802, 162; organized as a State, 162
Ohio troops first in the field in the War for Independence, 196, 199; surrendered to the British by Gen. Hull, 202, 203-204, 209, 213; Gen. Tupper's com., 217, 252, 266, 280, 294-296
Oliver, William, messenger, 181, 237
Ordinance of 1787, 44

Ottawa Towns, 213, 217
Ouiotenon, Ind., 64-66
Overton, Major, 226
Owens, Col. Theodore D., 253

P

Packet, Lieutenant, 296
Parsons, Samuel H., Judge, 44
Patriotism, absolution from, 207-208
Paul, Col. George, 252
Payne, General, 228
Peace Commissioners, 86; prisoners of the British, 88; report of, 91; for closing War of 1812, 302; overtures unavailing, 80, 82; victory of, 131; Wayne's last overture for, 111
Pennsylvania, savagery in, 79; troops from, 48, 54, 56, 216, 231
Perry, Oliver H., builds armed vessels, 263-273; captures all of Br. squadron, 269; aids invasion of Canada, 286; loses trophies in storm, 289; goes to Buffalo, 292
Perrysburg, Ohio, 230
Pickering, Timothy, 86
Pinckney, Thomas, 1st Minister to Great Britain, 31
Piqua, Ohio, 206
Pogue, Colonel, 215
Pontiac, 7, 79, 172
Population, of Michigan Ter. in 1811, 191; of Ohio Ter. in 1796 and 1800, 159; in 1802, 162
Poquette, Francis, slain, 159
Port Clinton, Ohio, 277
Porter, Capt. Moses, 148
Presque Isle, of Maumee River, 113, 223; of Maumee Bay, 229; Erie, Pa., 263
Prisoners, Am., 201, 227, 243; Br. 243, 260, 273, 289
Proclamations, of neutrality, 31, 100; for peace by Pennsylvania, Virginia, and Gen. Wayne, 81-82
Proctor, Col. Thomas, 63
Proctor, Col. and Gen. Henry A., Br., at Battle of the Raisin, 227; Siege of Fort Meigs, 235-239; at Fort Stephenson, 259; downfall at the Battle of the Thames, 288; asks more than he would accord to others, 292
Prophet, the Shawnee, 174-189
Put-in-Bay, Lake Erie, 266, 271
Put-in-Bay Island, 271, 296
Putnam, Gen. Rufus, 82

Q

Quebec, 227
Quincey, Josiah, opposed Louisiana purchase, 187

R

Raisin River, lesson of defeat at, 228
Randolph, Gov. Beverly, 62, 86
Refuge forts built, 85, 187, 205
Religious missionaries, 6, 159
Reports, from Am. mil. posts, 175-189; Gen. Gano, 294-296; Col. Hamtramck, 132-136; Peace Commissioners, 91, 95-96, 102, 112, 114, 116, 117, 127, 140
Reservations: for Aborigines, 170; for United States, 35
Revolutionary War, no peace after, 17; see under War
Reynolds, James, Surgeon's Mate, 200
Richardson, Br. Major, report of cannibalism, 230
Richardville, Chief Jean B., 134

Index

Rivers, along which the Aborigines lived, derived much of their food, and passed their happiest moments when not on the war-path: Auglaize, 75, 83–84, 90, 97, 105–106, 109, 111, 125, 169, 245; Blanchard, 197, 213, 217; Cuyahoga, 35, 39, 249; Detroit Strait, 267, see under Detroit; Eel, 65, 66, 82; Illinois, 164; Mad, 39; Maumee, 35, 49–51, 54–56, 59, 65–66, 75, 82, great councils by, 83–91, 101, 104–106, 109; excels in beauty, 110, great emporium of the hostiles, 110–111, 115, 118, 125, 128, 146, 164, 169, 196, 199, 207, 245; Miami, 37, 67, 125; Mississippi, discovery of, 1; navigation of, 39, 40, 99; Niagara, 263–264; Ohio, Rapids of, 45, 47–49, 65–66, 88–89, 98, 148, 164; Portage, 229, 252, 266; Raisin, battle and massacre at, 224–227, 291; Sandusky, 35, 128, 216; St. Clair Strait, 298, 301; St. Marys, 124, 208; Scioto, 81, 142, 174, 197; Swan Creek, 118, 119, 164; Thames, Canada, 286–287, 297; Tiffin, 110; Tippecanoe, 174, 190; Tuscarawas, 35; Wabash, 45, 48–49, 54, 64, 66, 68, 82, 154, 164; White, Ind., 153
Roads, treaty for, 171–172
Roche de Bout, Rock point, French landmark in Maumee River, 112, 145, 196

S

St. Clair, Arthur, 43; Gov. N. W. Ter., 44, 46, 49, 54–55, 63, 66; army, 67; defeat of, 68, 75, 81

St. Clair, Arthur, naval officer, 298
St. Marys, Ohio, 125, 208
Sandusky, Ohio, 181
Sargent, Winthrop, Sec. N. W. Ter., 44, 51, 151, 153; Gov. Miss. Ter., 156
Savages, allied to Br. against Americans, 11–17; massed with Br., 235; see, also, under Aborigines, Massacres, and Cannibalism
Scalps, bought of Savages, 6, 13, 282; exhibited to Br. to show effective work, 104
Schaumberg, Captain, 146, 154
Scott, Gen. Charles, 51, 62, 64–65; reinforces Wayne, 108, 122; Gov. of Kentucky, 205
Scott, Colonel, 207
Scott, Col., afterwards Gen., Winfield, 263
Settlements, 45; inefficient protection of, 60; receive impetus and stability, 160, 171; petition for protection 190–191
Shelby, Gen. Isaac, member Board of War, 62; Gov. of Kentucky, 277; with Harrison at Battle of the Thames, 289
Sickness: influenza (la grippe) in Wayne's army, 95–96; among the British and Savages, 119; in Winchester's army, 218–219; at Fort Meigs, 247
Siege, of Fort Wayne, 207–209; of Fort Meigs, 238–242; second investment, 251–255
Simcoe, Col. John Graves, Lieut.-Gov. Canada, 80, 86, 100; builds Ft. Miami by Maumee, 101, 114, 127–128
Sinclair, Capt. Patrick, Br. Com. Fort Mackinac, 15

Slaves, African, at Detroit, 191
Slocum, Charles E., *History of The Maumee River Basin*, 21, 136; on the six Forts Miami, 201
Slough, Captain, at St. Clair's defeat, 68
Smiley, Major, Expedition through Canada, 295
Spain, scheme to capture territory of, 43, offended by Jay Treaty, 152; builds forts in Am. territory, 153; abandons forts, 157; protection of against Br., 155; cedes Louisiana to France, 160
States organized, *see* under Civil Organizations
Steuben, Baron von, 23
Stewart, Commander, 196, 262
Stickney, Major Benjamin F., 193
Symmes, John C., Judge, 45

T

Tecumseh, Shawnee chief, conspiracy of with the "Prophet" and Br., 174, 182, 187, 189, 254; slain, 288
Temple, Sir John B., Br. consul, 27
Territories west of the Alleghany Mts.: N. W., 80, 144, 146, 156, 158; S. W. 141, 144, 156-157; *see* also, under Civil Organizations, Northwestern Territory, Ohio Country, and Union with U. S. Imperilled
Tiffin, Ohio, 217
Tories, loyalists, 30, 43, 93
Trading agencies for the Aborigines, 128, 177, 180, 182
Treaties, with Aborigines: 1784, 34; 1785, 35, 36; 1786, 37-38; 1789, 46; 1792, 82; 1795, 138-143; 1803, 163; 1804-05, 164-165; 1807, 168-170; 1808, 171-172; 1809, 178-179; 1814, 291; object of, 173
With Great Britain: 1783, at Paris, 18, 23, 24; 1794, by John Jay, 146; 1814, at Ghent, 302-307
With Spain, 1795, 144
Between France and Spain against the U. S., 1796, 152
With France, 1800, 160
Trimble, Major David, 237
Truman, Alexander, peace messenger, killed by the Savages, 82
Tryon, Gov. William, Br., 13
Tupper, S., agent, 177; Gen., 204, 217
Turner, Captain on Lake Huron, 300

U

Union with United States Imperilled, 40, 43-45, 152-154, 161, 166
United States beset on all sides, 98-99; *see* under Federalists; inefficiency of government of, 60-61; military posts held by Br. in, 23; reservations of land, 35, 138-143; troops of, 45, 48-49, 55-57, 67, 72, 96, 252-253, 262, 266
Upper Sandusky, Ohio, 217
Urbana, Ohio, 196, 204

V

Vance, Major, 295
Van Horn, Capt., wounded, 299
Varnum, James M., Judge, 44
Vincennes, 49, 179, 196
Virginia, cedes claim in Ohio Country to the U. S., 34; troops from, 48, 62, 216, 231; savagery in, 79

W

Walker, Lieut., slain, 234
War, Board of, 62
War of 1812, the War for Independence, 195; Independence assured, 307–308
Washington, George, General, 16, 23, 26; President, 44, 49, 58, 63, 75, 80–81, 84, 86, 100, 102; Lieut.-Gen., 157
Wayne, Gen. Anthony, chosen to lead third army against the Savages, 81, 83–84; reports to Sec. of War, 95–96, 102, 112, 114, 116, 117, 127, 140; meets hydra of opposition, 100; is caught under falling tree, 109; at Battle of Fallen Timber, 113; makes treaty at Greenville, 138–143; death of, 149, 150
Wells, Capt. William, 175, 201; murdered and eaten, 202
Western confederacy advocated, 40, 43–45, 152–154, 161, 165–166
Western Reserve, Connecticut's, 39, 158, 164
Wilkinson, Gen. James, 43, 64, 66–67, 76, 82, 97; succeeds Gen. Wayne, 146, 148, 157
Williams, General, 149
Winchester, Gen. James, 206–207; great sufferings of his army at Defiance, 218–220, 222–223; army destroyed at the Raisin, 224–226
Wood, Capt., builds Fort Meigs, 230–231
Worthington, Thomas, 198, 202
Wyllys, Major, slain, 57

Z

Zeisberger, Rev. David, diary quoted, 21

www.ingramcontent.com/pod-product-compliance
Lightning Source LLC
Chambersburg PA
CBHW070934230426
43666CB00011B/2437